DOVER · THRIFT · EDITIONS

Women's Wit and Wisdom

A Book of Quotations

EDITED BY

SUSAN L. RATTINER

DOVER PUBLICATIONS, INC.
Mineola, New York

DOVER THRIFT EDITIONS

GENERAL EDITOR: PAUL NEGRI
EDITOR OF THIS VOLUME: SUSAN L. RATTINER

DEDICATION

This book is lovingly dedicated to my parents,
Myrna and Alan Rattiner.

This one's for you, Ma.

Bibliographical Note

Women's Wit and Wisdom: A Book of Quotations is a new work, first published by Dover Publications, Inc., in 2000.

Library of Congress Cataloging-in-Publication Data

Women's wit and wisdom : a book of quotations / edited by Susan L. Rattiner.
    p. cm. — (Dover thrift editions)
    ISBN 0-486-41123-0 (pbk.)
    1. Women—Quotations. 2. Quotations, English. I. Rattiner, Susan L. II. Series.

PN6081.5 .W59 2000
305.4—dc21

00-022782

Manufactured in the United States of America
Dover Publications, Inc., 31 East 2nd Street, Mineola, N.Y. 11501

Note

Women, from antiquity to the present day, have addressed a multitude of issues with clarity and enduring vision. Contrary to what has often been believed, their observations, objections, and exhortations concerning their role in society—and life in general—can be found throughout history. While in earlier eras most women hesitated to voice their opinions for fear of censure, there were always a select few who boldly spoke out, obliterating gender barriers with their wit and wisdom, and blazing a trail for other women to follow. These early persevering women—and their many successors—are inspirations to us all, women and men alike.

The quotations in this book, selected from literature, speeches, poetry, and other sources, often display a remarkable continuity of thought, proving that certain prevailing attitudes are not innovations after all. Marriage as an institution carried a pejorative connotation for Fanny Burney, who referred to it in 1768 as the "end to a woman's liberty"— to many a 20th-century sentiment. In a poem published in 1894, Frances Ellen Watkins Harper laments the "double standard" that precludes gender equality: "And what is wrong in woman's life / In man's cannot be right."

Most of the authors in this book are famous novelists, celebrities, and public figures, including Christina Rossetti, Jane Austen, and Eleanor Roosevelt. Others, such as Margaret Wolfe Hungerford and Mary Delarivier Manley, are lesser known writers, but the impact of their words has left a lasting impression for generations: "Beauty is in the eye of the beholder" and "No time like the present," respectively. Although there are a variety of differing opinions offered here, many of which consist of opposing views, it is especially interesting to listen to the echo of the women of yesterday in the voices of the women of today.

The variety and vitality of women's thought is the primary focus of this compilation. From the sensible to the outrageous, the sayings of women, ranging from ancient times to the 20th century, pertain to all aspects of life. One proviso for the reader, however, is to remember that these quotations are not spliced out of time, but possess a historical context that must be kept in mind. In an uncanny forecasting of the future, for example, author and social reformer Lydia Maria Child predicted that she would not live to see women allowed to vote; she died in 1880 (forty years before the 19th Amendment gave women the right to vote). The quotations presented here are divided into subject categories and arranged chronologically by the author's date of birth. Sources and dates have been cited for each quotation (where possible).

Contents

Women   1

Men   4

Love and Romance   7

Marriage   12

Family: Mother, Father, Siblings   15

Children   17

Household   19

Human Nature   20

Friendship   24

Aging   25

Life   27

Death   31

Truth, Honesty, Secrets, and Lies   33

Self-Esteem and Self-Evaluation   35

Success, Ambition, Achievement,
    and Dreams   38

Injustice and Prejudice; Freedom
    and Racial Harmony   41

Quest for Gender Equality   43

Education and Intelligence   45

Work and Occupations   46

Wealth and Money   50

Joy and Sorrow   52

Writing   53

Language, the Arts, and Criticism   55

Nature, the Environment, and Time   57

Culture and Politics   60

Various Subjects / Miscellaneous   62

Index of Authors   65

WOMEN

I am obnoxious to each carping tongue,
Who says my hand a needle better fits,
A poet's pen, all scorn, I should thus wrong.
ANNE BRADSTREET c. 1612–1672; "The Prologue" (1678)

%

How much it is to be regretted, that the British ladies should ever sit down contented to polish, when they are able to reform; to entertain, when they might instruct; and to dazzle for an hour, when they are candidates for eternity!
HANNAH MORE 1745–1833; "On Dissipation,"
Essays on Various Subjects . . . for Young Ladies (1777)

%

I do not wish them [women] to have power over men; but over themselves.
MARY WOLLSTONECRAFT 1759–1797;
A Vindication of the Rights of Woman (1792)

%

A man can brave opinion, a woman must submit to it.
MADAME DE STAËL 1766–1817; *Delphine* (1802)

%

Reason and religion teach us that we too are primary existences, that it is for us to move in the orbit of our duty around the holy center of perfection, the companions not the satellites of men.
EMMA HART WILLARD 1787–1870;
inscribed in the Hall of Fame of Great Americans, n.d.

1

Woman stock is rising in the market. I shall not live to see women vote, but I'll come and rap at the ballot box.

LYDIA MARIA CHILD 1802–1880; letter to Sarah Shaw
(August 3, 1856)

❧

Thou large-brained woman and large-hearted man.

ELIZABETH BARRETT BROWNING 1806–1861;
"To George Sand—A Desire" (1844)

❧

I should like to know what is the proper function of women, if it is not to make reasons for husbands to stay at home, and still stronger reasons for bachelors to go out.

GEORGE ELIOT [MARY ANN EVANS] 1819–1880;
The Mill on the Floss (1860)

❧

Half the sorrows of women would be averted if they could repress the speech they know to be useless; nay, the speech they have resolved not to make.

GEORGE ELIOT [MARY ANN EVANS] 1819–1880;
Felix Holt (1866)

❧

". . . women have been called queens for a long time, but the kingdom given them isn't worth ruling."

LOUISA MAY ALCOTT 1832–1888; *An Old-Fashioned Girl* (1869)

❧

No woman can call herself free who does not own and control her body. No woman can call herself free until she can choose consciously whether she will or will not be a mother.

MARGARET SANGER 1883–1966;
Woman and the New Race (1920)

❧

Shall we watch in patience the murdering of 25,000 women each year in the United States from criminal abortions? Shall we fold our hands and wait until a body of sleek and well-fed politicians get ready to abolish the cause of such slaughter?

MARGARET SANGER 1883–1966;
My Fight for Birth Control (1931)

I am a woman, I am weak,
  And custom leads me as one blind,
Only my songs go where they will
  Free as the wind.
                SARA TEASDALE 1884–1933; "The Wind," *Love Songs* (1917)

&

A woman will always have to be better than a man in any job she undertakes.
                ELEANOR ROOSEVELT 1884–1962; *My Day* (Nov. 29, 1945)

&

A woman is like a tea bag. You never know how strong she is until she gets into hot water.
          ELEANOR ROOSEVELT 1884–1962; this quotation has also been attributed
                to NANCY REAGAN (b. 1923) in *Observer* (March 29, 1981),
                    slightly reworded as "A woman is like a tea bag—
                      only in hot water do you realize how strong she is."

&

I was, being human, born alone;
I am, being woman, hard beset.
                            ELINOR WYLIE 1885–1928;
                    "Let No Charitable Hope," *Black Armour* (1923)

&

All the tired women,
  Who sewed their lives away,
Speak in my deft fingers
  As I sew today.
              HAZEL HALL 1886–1924; "Instruction," (1922)

&

Whatever women do they must do twice as well as men to be thought half as good.
                        CHARLOTTE WHITTON 1896–1975;
                        Canada Month (June 1963)

&

Women have no wilderness in them,
They are provident instead,
Content in the tight hot cell of their hearts
To eat dusty bread.
                    LOUISE BOGAN 1897–1970; "Women" (1923)

But if God had wanted us to think just with our wombs, why did He give us a brain?

CLARE BOOTH LUCE 1903–1987; *Life* (October 16, 1970)

ॐ

One is not born a woman: one becomes one.

SIMONE DE BEAUVOIR 1908–1986; *Le deuxième sexe* (1949)

ॐ

Women want men, careers, money, children, friends, luxury, comfort, independence, freedom, respect, love, and a three-dollar pantyhose that won't run.

PHYLLIS DILLER b. 1917; in Ashton Applewhite (ed.),
And I Quote (1992)

ॐ

In politics, if you want anything said, ask a man. If you want anything done, ask a woman.

MARGARET THATCHER b. 1925; (said in 1970)

ॐ

A liberated woman is one who has sex before marriage and a job after.

GLORIA STEINEM b. 1934; *Newsweek* (March 28, 1960)

ॐ

Let's face it, there are no plain women on television.

ANNA FORD b. 1943; *Observer* (September 23, 1979)

MEN

The more I see of men, the better I like dogs.

MARIE-JEANNE ROLAND 1754–1793; attributed

ॐ

Man is to be held only by the *slightest* chains, with the idea that he can break them at pleasure, he submits to them in sport.

MARIA EDGEWORTH 1768–1849;
Letters for Literary Ladies (1795)

Men have had every advantage of us in telling their own story. Education has been theirs in so much higher a degree; the pen has been in their hands.

JANE AUSTEN 1775–1817; *Persuasion* (1818)

❧

Men for the sake of getting a living forget to live.

MARGARET FULLER 1810–1850; *Summer on the Lakes* (1844)

❧

A man . . . is *so* in the way in the house!

ELIZABETH GASKELL 1810–1865; *Cranford* (1853)

❧

A man is seldom ashamed of feeling that he cannot love a woman so well when he sees a certain greatness in her: nature having intended greatness for men.

GEORGE ELIOT [MARY ANN EVANS] 1819–1880;
Middlemarch (1871–2)

❧

Blessed is the man who, having nothing to say, abstains from giving us wordy evidence of the fact.

GEORGE ELIOT [MARY ANN EVANS] 1819–1880;
Theophrastus Such (1878)

❧

A gentleman opposed to their enfranchisement once said to me, "Women have never produced anything of any value to the world." I told him the chief product of the women had been the men, and left it to him to decide whether the product was of any value.

ANNA HOWARD SHAW 1847–1919; address to the
National Woman Suffrage Association (April 29, 1899)

❧

"Instead of always harping on a man's faults, tell him of his virtues. Try to pull him out of his rut of bad habits. Hold up to him his better self, his *real* self that can dare and do and win out . . . People radiate what is in their minds and in their hearts."

ELEANOR H. PORTER 1868–1920; *Pollyanna* (1912)

It takes a woman twenty years to make a man of her son, and another woman twenty minutes to make a fool of him.

HELEN ROWLAND 1875–1950;
Reflections of a Bachelor Girl (1903)

ᵌ➐

The follies which a man regrets most, in his life, are those which he didn't commit when he had the opportunity.

HELEN ROWLAND 1875–1950; *A Guide to Men* (1922)

ᵌ➐

Somehow a bachelor never quite gets over the idea that he is a thing of beauty and a boy forever.

HELEN ROWLAND 1875–1950; *A Guide to Men* (1922)

ᵌ➐

I never liked the men I loved, and never loved the men I liked.

FANNY BRICE 1891–1951; in Norman Katkov,
The Fabulous Fanny (1952)

ᵌ➐

A man in the house is worth two in the street.

MAE WEST 1892–1980; *Belle of the Nineties* (1934)

ᵌ➐

The best way to hold a man is in your arms.

MAE WEST 1892–1980;
in Joseph Weintraub, *Peel Me a Grape* (1975)

ᵌ➐

A hard man is good to find.

MAE WEST 1892–1980; attributed

ᵌ➐

There is, of course, no reason for the existence of the male sex except that sometimes one needs help with moving the piano.

REBECCA WEST 1892–1983;
Sunday Telegraph (June 28, 1970)

. . . I had been fed, in my youth, a lot of old wives' tales about the way men would instantly forsake a beautiful woman to flock around a brilliant one. It is but fair to say that, after getting out in the world, I had never seen this happen.

DOROTHY PARKER 1893–1967; *Constant Reader* (1970)

❧

Women want mediocre men, and men are working hard to be as mediocre as possible.

MARGARET MEAD 1901–1978;
Quote Magazine (June 15, 1958)

❧

If men could get pregnant, abortion would be a sacrament.

FLORYNCE KENNEDY b. 1916; said in 1970;
Ms. magazine (March 1973)

❧

Men decided a few centuries ago that any job they found repulsive was women's work.

FRANCES GABE; said in 1983;
in Anne L. MacDonald, *Feminine Ingenuity* (1992)

❧

My ancestors wandered lost in the wilderness for 40 years because even in biblical times, men would not stop to ask for directions.

ELAYNE BOOSLER b. 1952; *Time* (Fall 1990)

LOVE AND ROMANCE

Love—bittersweet, irrepressible—
loosens my limbs and I tremble.

SAPPHO c. 613–580 B.C.; "To Atthis" (6th Century B.C.);
in Willis Barnstone, *Sappho* (1965)

Love made me poet,
And this I writ;
My heart did do it,
And not my wit.

> ELIZABETH, LADY TANFIELD c. 1565–1628;
> epitaph for her husband

❧

Love ceases to be a pleasure, when it ceases to be a secret.

> APHRA BEHN 1640–1689; *The Lover's Watch* (1686)

❧

Oh, what a dear ravishing thing is the beginning of an Amour!

> APHRA BEHN 1640–1689; *The Emperor of the Moon* (1687)

❧

Nothing to be done without a bribe I find, in love as well as law.

> SUSANNAH CENTLIVRE c. 1669–1723;
> *The Perjured Husband* (1700)

❧

The cure of a romantic first flame is a better surety to subsequent discretion, than all the exhortations of all the fathers, and mothers, and guardians, and maiden aunts in the universe.

> FANNY BURNEY 1752–1840; *Camilla* (1796)

❧

No riches from his scanty store
My lover could impart;
He gave a boon I valued more,
He gave me all his heart.

> HELEN MARIA WILLIAMS 1762–1827;
> "Song," *An Ode to Peace and Other Poems* (1782–1788)

❧

In nine cases out of ten, a woman had better show *more* affection than she feels.

> JANE AUSTEN 1775–1817; *Pride and Prejudice* (1813)

❧

May I ask whether these pleasing attentions proceed from the impulse of the moment, or are the result of previous study?

> JANE AUSTEN 1775–1817; *Pride and Prejudice* (1813)

I sometimes think the gods have united human beings by some mysterious principle, like the according notes of music. Or is it as Plato has supposed, that souls originally one have been divided, and each seeks the half it lost?

LYDIA MARIA CHILD 1802–1880; *Philothea: A Romance* (1836)

≥●

"Yes," I answered you last night;
"No," this morning, sir, I say.
Colours seen by candle-light
Will not look the same by day.

ELIZABETH BARRETT BROWNING 1806–1861;
"The Lady's Yes" (1844)

≥●

How do I love thee? Let me count the ways.
I love thee to the depth and breadth and height
My soul can reach.

ELIZABETH BARRETT BROWNING 1806–1861;
Sonnets from the Portuguese (1850)

≥●

He woos me with those honeyed words
That women love to hear.

EMMA C. EMBURY 1806–1863; "The Widow's Wooer" (c. 1860)

≥●

The way to a man's heart is through his stomach.

FANNY FERN [SARA PAYSON WILLIS] 1811–1872;
Willis Parton n.d.

≥●

My love for Linton is like the foliage in the woods; time will change it, I'm well aware, as winter changes the trees—My love for Heathcliff resembles the eternal rocks beneath:—a source of little visible delight, but necessary.

EMILY BRONTË 1818–1848; *Wuthering Heights* (1847)

≥●

A difference of taste in jokes is a great strain on the affections.

GEORGE ELIOT [MARY ANN EVANS] 1819–1880;
Daniel Deronda (1876)

Intense love is often akin to intense suffering.

> FRANCES ELLEN WATKINS HARPER 1825–1911;
> "The Two Offers," *Anglo-African Magazine* (1859)

&

We don't believe in rheumatism and true love until after the first attack.

> MARIE VON EBNER-ESCHENBACH 1830–1916; *Aphorism* (1905)

&

The fate of love is that it always seems too little or too much.

> AMELIA E. BARR 1831–1919; *The Belle of Bowling Green* (1904)

&

I believe love, pure and true,
Is to the soul a sweet, immortal dew.

> MARY ASHLEY TOWNSEND 1832–1901;
> "Creed," *Down the Bayou and Other Poems* (1881)

&

I am as weak as other women are—
Your frown can make the whole world like a tomb.

> ELLA WHEELER WILCOX 1850–1919;
> "Individuality," *Poems of Passion* (1883)

&

Love, the strongest and deepest element in all life, the harbinger of hope, of joy, of ecstasy; love, the defier of all laws, of all conventions; love, the freest, the most powerful molder of human destiny; how can such an all-compelling force be synonymous with that poor little State- and Church-begotten weed, marriage?

> EMMA GOLDMAN 1869–1940;
> *Anarchism and Other Essays* (1911)

&

So blind is life, so long at last is sleep,
And none but Love to bid us laugh or weep.

> WILLA CATHER 1873–1947;
> "Evening Song," *April Twilights* (1903)

&

And the softness of my body will be guarded from embrace
By each button, hook, and lace.

> AMY LOWELL 1874–1925; "Patterns," (1916)

You are ice and fire,
The touch of you burns my hands like snow.

> AMY LOWELL 1874–1925;
> "Opal," *Pictures of the Floating World* (1919)

❧

An impersonal and scientific knowledge of the structure of our bodies
is the surest safeguard against prurient curiosity and lascivious gloating.

> MARIE STOPES 1880–1958; *Married Love* (1918)

❧

Passion always goes, and boredom stays.

> GABRIELLE "COCO" CHANEL 1883–1971;
> in Frances Kennett,
> *Coco: the Life and Loves of Gabrielle Chanel* (1989)

❧

For though I know he loves me,
    To-night my heart is sad;
His kiss was not so wonderful
    As all the dreams I had.

> SARA TEASDALE 1884–1933; "The Kiss," *Love Songs* (1917)

❧

Never think she loves him wholly,
Never believe her love is blind,
All his faults are locked securely
In a closet of her mind.

> SARA TEASDALE 1884–1933; "Appraisal," *Dark of the Moon* (1926)

❧

Your thorns are the best part of you.

> MARIANNE MOORE 1887–1972; "Roses Only," *Others* (1917)

❧

Pity me that the heart is slow to learn
What the swift mind beholds at every turn.

> EDNA ST. VINCENT MILLAY 1892–1950; "Pity Me Not" (1922)

❧

Men seldom make passes
At girls who wear glasses.

> DOROTHY PARKER 1893–1967;
> "News Item" (1926) in *Not So Deep as a Well* (1937)

I'm as pure as the driven slush.

> TALLULAH BANKHEAD 1903–1968;
> *Saturday Evening Post* (April 12, 1947)

MARRIAGE

A father will have compassion on his son. A mother will never forget her child. A brother will cover the sin of his sister. But what husband ever forgave the faithlessness of his wife?

> MARGUERITE OF NAVARRE 1492–1549;
> *Mirror of the Sinful Soul* (1531)

❧

I do not want a husband who honours me as a queen, if he does not love me as a woman.

> ELIZABETH I 1533–1603; in Frederick Chamberlin,
> *The Sayings of Queen Elizabeth* (1923)

❧

If ever two were one, then surely we.

> ANNE BRADSTREET c. 1612–1672;
> "To My Dear and Loving Husband" (c. 1650)

❧

Wife and servant are the same,
But only differ in the name.

> LADY MARY CHUDLEIGH 1656–1710;
> "To the Ladies," *Poems on Several Occasions* (1703)

❧

O! how short a time does it take to put an end to a woman's liberty!

> FANNY BURNEY 1752–1840; diary (July 1768)

❧

No man is in love when he marries . . . There is something in the formalities of the matrimonial preparations that drive away all the little cupidons.

> FANNY BURNEY 1752–1840; *Camilla* (1796)

"From this day you must be a stranger to one of your parents.—Your mother will never see you again if you do *not* marry Mr. Collins, and I will never see you again if you *do*."

> JANE AUSTEN 1775–1817; *Pride and Prejudice* (1813)

ಈ

Happiness in marriage is entirely a matter of chance.

> JANE AUSTEN 1775–1817; *Pride and Prejudice* (1813)

ಈ

Even quarrels with one's husband are preferable to the ennui of a solitary existence.

> ELIZABETH PATTERSON BONAPARTE 1785–1879;
> in Eugene L. Didier,
> *The Life and Letters of Madame Bonaparte* (1879)

ಈ

A woman dictates before marriage in order that she may have an appetite for submission afterwards.

> GEORGE ELIOT [MARY ANN EVANS] 1819–1880;
> *Middlemarch* (1871–2)

ಈ

A woman, let her be as good as she may, has got to put up with the life her husband makes for her.

> GEORGE ELIOT [MARY ANN EVANS] 1819–1880;
> *Middlemarch* (1871–2)

ಈ

I do not consider divorce an evil by any means. It is just as much a refuge for women married to brutal men as Canada was to the slaves of brutal masters.

> SUSAN B. ANTHONY 1820–1906; in Ida Husted Harper,
> *The Life and Work of Susan B. Anthony* (1898)

ಈ

I do not consider, as it is so often stated, that the great object of marriage is to produce children; marriage has higher humanitarian objects.

> DR. ELIZABETH BLACKWELL 1821–1910;
> *How to Keep a Household in Health* (1870)

One of the trials of woman-kind is the fear of being an old maid. To escape this dreadful doom, young girls rush into matrimony with a recklessness which astonishes the beholder; never pausing to remember that the loss of liberty, happiness, and self-respect is poorly repaid by the barren honor of being called "Mrs." instead of "Miss."

> LOUISA MAY ALCOTT 1832–1888; "Happy Women,"
> *The New York Ledger* (April 11, 1868)

❧

A literary woman's best critic is her husband . . .

> ELIZABETH STUART PHELPS 1844–1911;
> *Chapters from a Life* (1897)

❧

The reason that husbands and wives do not understand each other is because they belong to different sexes.

> DOROTHY DIX 1861–1951; syndicated column

❧

When you see what some girls marry, you realize how they must hate to work for a living.

> HELEN ROWLAND 1875–1950;
> *Reflections of a Bachelor Girl* (1909)

❧

A husband is what is left of a lover, after the nerve has been extracted.

> HELEN ROWLAND 1875–1950; *A Guide to Men* (1922)

❧

When a girl marries, she exchanges the attentions of many men for the inattention of one.

> HELEN ROWLAND 1875–1950; in Robert Byrne (ed.),
> *1,911 Best Things Anybody Ever Said* (1988)

❧

I married beneath me, all women do.

> NANCY ASTOR 1879–1964;
> in *Dictionary of National Biography* (1981)

❧

The true male never yet walked
Who liked to listen when his mate talked.

> ANNA WICKHAM 1884–1947;
> "The Affinity," *The Contemplative Quarry* (1915)

Marriage always demands the greatest understanding of the art of insincerity possible between two human beings.

> VICKI BAUM 1888–1960; *And Life Goes On* (1931)

❧

An archaeologist is the best husband a woman can have; the older she gets, the more interested he is in her.

> AGATHA CHRISTIE 1891–1976; who was married to one;
> in Robert Byrne (ed.), *1,911 Best Things Anybody Ever Said*
> (1988)

❧

A man in love is incomplete until he has married. Then he's finished.

> ZSA ZSA GABOR b. 1919; *Newsweek* (March 28, 1960)

❧

Never marry a man who hates his mother, because he'll end up hating you.

> JILL BENNETT 1931–1990; *Observer* (September 1982)

❧

If you hear of me getting married, slap me.

> ELIZABETH TAYLOR b. 1932; television interview, *20/20* (1997)

❧

There were three of us in this marriage, so it was a bit crowded.

> DIANA, PRINCESS OF WALES 1961–1997;
> television interview (November 1995)

FAMILY: MOTHER, FATHER, SIBLINGS

A slavish bondage to parents cramps every faculty of the mind.

> MARY WOLLSTONECRAFT 1759–1797;
> *A Vindication of the Rights of Woman* (1792)

❧

Who ran to help me when I fell,
And would some pretty story tell,
Or kiss the place to make it well?
  My Mother.

> ANN TAYLOR 1782–1866; "My Mother," in Jane Taylor
> and Her Sisters, *Original Poems for Infant Minds* (1804)

No music is so pleasant to my ears as that word—father.
> LYDIA MARIA CHILD 1802–1880; *Philothea: A Romance* (1836)

৯

Over the river, and through the wood,
To grandfather's house we go.
> LYDIA MARIA CHILD 1802–1880; "The New-England Boy's
> Song About Thanksgiving Day" (1857)

৯

To her the name of father was another name for love.
> FANNY FERN [SARA PAYSON WILLIS] 1811–1872;
> *Fresh Leaves* (1857)

৯

The mother's yearning, that completest type of the life in another life which is the essence of real human love, feels the presence of the cherished child even in the debased, degraded man.
> GEORGE ELIOT [MARY ANN EVANS] 1819–1880; *Adam Bede* (1859)

৯

For there is no friend like a sister
In calm or stormy weather;
To cheer one on the tedious way,
To fetch one if one goes astray,
To lift one if one totters down,
To strengthen whilst one stands.
> CHRISTINA ROSSETTI 1830–1894; "Goblin Market" (1862)

৯

". . . It's a great comfort to have an artistic sister."
> LOUISA MAY ALCOTT 1832–1888; *Little Women* (1868)

৯

My dear father; my dear friend; the best and wisest man I ever knew; who taught me many lessons and showed me many things as we went together along the country by-ways.
> SARAH ORNE JEWETT 1849–1909;
> dedication to *Country By-Ways* (1881)

৯

A mother is not a person to lean on but a person to make leaning unnecessary.
> DOROTHY CANFIELD FISHER 1879–1958; *Her Son's Wife* (1926)

Family jokes, though rightly cursed by strangers, are the bond that keeps most families alive.

STELLA BENSON 1892–1933; *Pipers and a Dancer* (1924)

≈

To describe my mother would be to write about a hurricane in its perfect power.

MAYA ANGELOU b. 1928;
I Know Why the Caged Bird Sings (1970)

≈

I have reached the age when a woman begins to perceive that she is growing into the person she least plans to resemble: her mother.

ANITA BROOKNER b. 1938; *Incidents in the Rue Laugier* (1995)

≈

Biology is the least of what makes someone a mother.

OPRAH WINFREY b. 1953; *Woman's Day* (1988)

CHILDREN

These are all the jewels of which I can boast.

CORNELIA fl.160–140 B.C.; of her two sons; in Sarah Josepha
Hale, *Biography of Distinguished Women* (1876)

≈

A child's a plaything for an hour.

MARY ANN LAMB 1764–1847; *Parental Recollections*, n.d.

≈

I s'pect I growed. Don't think nobody never made me.

HARRIET BEECHER STOWE 1811–1896;
Uncle Tom's Cabin (1852)

≈

You will find as the children grow up that as a rule children are a bitter disappointment—their greatest object being to do precisely what their parents do not wish and have anxiously tried to prevent.

QUEEN VICTORIA 1819–1901; letter to the Crown Prince
of Prussia (January 5, 1876)

Just as everybody has the vote including women, I think children should, because as a child is conscious of itself then it has to me an existence and has a stake in what happens.

> GERTRUDE STEIN 1874–1946; said in 1946;
> in Robert Haas, *What Are Masterpieces* (1970)

I think, at a child's birth, if a mother could ask a fairy godmother to endow it with the most useful gift, that gift would be curiosity.

> ELEANOR ROOSEVELT 1884–1962; *Today's Health* (October 1966)

Childhood is not from birth to a certain age and at a certain age
The child is grown, and puts away childish things.
Childhood is the kingdom where nobody dies.

> EDNA ST. VINCENT MILLAY 1892–1950; "Childhood Is the
> Kingdom Where Nobody Dies" (1934)

There is no end to the violations committed by children on children, quietly talking alone.

> ELIZABETH BOWEN 1899–1973; *The House in Paris* (1935)

Death and taxes and childbirth! There's never any convenient time for any of them.

> MARGARET MITCHELL 1900–1949; *Gone with the Wind* (1936)

If from infancy you treat children as gods they are liable in adulthood to act as devils.

> P. D. JAMES b. 1920; *The Children of Men* (1992)

If you bungle raising your children, I don't think whatever else you do well matters very much.

> JACQUELINE KENNEDY ONASSIS 1929–1994;
> in Theodore C. Sorenson, *Kennedy* (1965)

Parents of young children should realize that few people, and maybe no one, will find their children as enchanting as they do.

> BARBARA WALTERS b. 1931; *How to Talk with Practically
> Anybody About Practically Anything* (1970)

HOUSEHOLD

A place for everything and everything in its place.

> MRS. BEETON 1836–1865;
> *The Book of Household Management* (1861)

કⁱ

The labor of women in the house, certainly, enables men to produce more wealth than they otherwise could; and in this way women are economic factors in society. But so are horses.

> CHARLOTTE PERKINS GILMAN 1860–1935;
> *Women and Economics* (1898)

ક

The fact that women in the home have shut themselves away from the thought and life of the world has done much to retard progress. We fill the world with the children of 20th century A.D. fathers and 20th century B.C. mothers.

> CHARLOTTE PERKINS GILMAN 1860–1935;
> in Ida Husted Harper, *History of Woman Suffrage* (1923)

ક

Let woman out of the home, let man into it, should be the aim of education. The home needs man, and the world outside needs woman.

> PEARL S. BUCK 1892–1973; *Of Men and Women* (1941)

ક

Hatred of domestic work is a natural and admirable result of civilization.

> REBECCA WEST 1892–1983; *The Freewoman* (June 6, 1912)

ક

By and large, mothers and housewives are the only workers who do not have regular time off. They are the great vacationless class.

> ANNE MORROW LINDBERGH b. 1906; *Gift from the Sea* (1955)

ક

I think housework is the reason most women go to the office.

> HELOISE CRUSE 1919–1977;
> *Editor and Publisher* (April 27, 1963)

Home is where you come to when you have nothing better to do.
MARGARET THATCHER b. 1925; *Vanity Fair* (May 1991)

HUMAN NATURE

When anger spreads through the breast, guard thy tongue from barking idly.
SAPPHO c. 610–635 B.C.; untitled fragment,
in Amelia Gere Mason, *Women in the Golden Ages* (1901)

❧

Courage is relaxed by delay.
ALDRUDE fl. 1170s; in Sarah Josepha Hale,
Biography of Distinguished Women (1876)

❧

Avarice breeds envy, a worm that is always gnawing, letting the avaricious enjoy neither their own nor anyone else's good.
ST. CATHERINE OF SIENA 1347–1380;
in Suzanne Noffke, tr., *Dialogue* (1378)

❧

A clear and innocent conscience fears nothing.
ELIZABETH I 1533–1603; in Frederick Chamberlin,
The Sayings of Queen Elizabeth (1923)

❧

A fool too late bewares when all the peril is past.
ELIZABETH I 1533–1603; in Frederick Chamberlin,
The Sayings of Queen Elizabeth (1923)

❧

Endeavour to be innocent as a dove, but as wise as a serpent.
ANN FANSHAWE 1625–1680; *Memoirs of Ann, Lady Fanshawe*
(c. 1670)

❧

There is nothing upon the face of the earth so insipid as a medium. Give me love or hate! a friend that will go to jail for me, or an enemy that will run me through the body!
FANNY BURNEY 1752–1840; *Camilla* (1796)

To be totally understanding makes one very indulgent.
MADAME DE STAËL 1766–1817;
Corinne (1807)

❧

The sooner every party breaks up the better.
JANE AUSTEN 1775–1817; *Emma* (1816)

❧

Every man is surrounded by a neighborhood of voluntary spies.
JANE AUSTEN 1775–1817;
Northanger Abbey (1818)

❧

It was, perhaps, one of those cases in which advice is good or bad only as the event decides.
JANE AUSTEN 1775–1817; *Persuasion* (1818)

❧

The best way to get the better of temptation is just to yield to it.
CLEMENTINA STIRLING GRAHAM 1782–1877;
Mystifications (1859)

❧

Persecution for opinion is the master vice of society.
FRANCES WRIGHT 1795–1852;
Course of Popular Lectures (1829)

❧

The devil's most devilish when respectable.
ELIZABETH BARRETT BROWNING 1806–1861;
Aurora Leigh (1857)

❧

Human nature is above all things—lazy.
HARRIET BEECHER STOWE 1811–1896;
Household Papers and Stories (1864)

❧

Cruelty, like every other vice, requires no motive outside itself—it only requires opportunity.
GEORGE ELIOT [MARY ANN EVANS] 1819–1880;
Scenes from a Clerical Life (1858)

Nothing is so good as it seems beforehand.
GEORGE ELIOT [MARY ANN EVANS] 1819–1880;
Silas Marner (1861)

☙

Gossip is a sort of smoke that comes from the dirty tobacco-pipes of those who diffuse it: it proves nothing but the bad taste of the smoker.
GEORGE ELIOT [MARY ANN EVANS] 1819–1880;
Daniel Deronda (1876)

☙

. . . people are almost always better than their neighbours think they are.
GEORGE ELIOT [MARY ANN EVANS] 1819–1880;
Middlemarch (1871–2)

☙

Fear not those who argue but those who dodge.
MARIE VON EBNER-ESCHENBACH 1830–1916; *Aphorism* (1905)

☙

All changes are more or less tinged with melancholy, for what we are leaving behind is part of ourselves.
AMELIA E. BARR 1831–1919; *All the Days of My Life* (1913)

☙

In the whole round of human affairs little is so fatal to peace as misunderstanding.
MARGARET E. SANGSTER 1838–1912;
An Autobiography from My Youth (1909)

☙

Indifference is the invincible giant of the world.
OUIDA [MARIE LOUISE DE LA RAMÉE] 1839–1908;
Wisdom, Wit and Pathos (1884)

☙

Sometimes a neighbor whom we have disliked a lifetime for his arrogance and conceit lets fall a single commonplace remark that shows us another side, another man, really; a man uncertain, and puzzled, and in the dark like ourselves.
WILLA CATHER 1873–1947; *Shadows on the Rock* (1931)

Science may have found a cure for most evils; but it has found no remedy for the worst of them all—the apathy of human beings.

HELEN KELLER 1880–1968; *My Religion* (1927)

❧

When one door of happiness closes another opens; but often we look so long at the closed door that we do not see the one which has been opened for us.

HELEN KELLER 1880–1968; *We Bereaved* (1929)

❧

. . . all big changes in human history have been arrived at slowly and through many compromises.

ELEANOR ROOSEVELT 1884–1962; said in 1925

❧

If you haven't got anything good to say about anyone come and sit by me.

ALICE ROOSEVELT LONGWORTH 1884–1980;
in Michael Teague, *Mrs. L: Conversations
with Alice Roosevelt Longworth* (1981)

❧

Human beings do not carry civilization in their genes. All that we do carry in our genes are certain capacities—the capacity to learn to walk upright, to use our brains, to speak, to relate to our fellow men, to construct and use tools, to explore the universe, and to express that exploration in religion, in art, in science, in philosophy.

MARGARET MEAD 1901–1978; "Human Nature Will Flower
If—" in the *New York Times Magazine* (April 19, 1964)

❧

The biggest disease today is not leprosy or tuberculosis, but rather the feeling of being unwanted, uncared for and deserted by everybody.

MOTHER TERESA 1910–1997;
Observer (October 3, 1971)

❧

We need to haunt the halls of history and listen anew to the ancestors' wisdom.

MAYA ANGELOU b. 1928; n.d.

Polite conversation is rarely either.

FRAN LEBOWITZ b. 1950;
Social Studies (1981)

FRIENDSHIP

Friendship's a noble name, 'tis love refined.

SUSANNAH CENTLIVRE c. 1667–1723;
The Stolen Heiress (1702)

❧

"Do you come to the play without knowing what it is?" "O yes, Sir, yes, very frequently; I have no time to read play-bills; one merely comes to meet one's friends, and show that one's alive."

FANNY BURNEY 1752–1840; *Evelina* (1778)

❧

Mary had a little lamb,
Its fleece was white as snow;
And everywhere that Mary went,
The lamb was sure to go.

SARAH JOSEPHA HALE 1788–1879; "Mary's Lamb,"
Poems for Our Children (1830)

❧

Friendships begin with liking or gratitude—roots that can be pulled up.

GEORGE ELIOT [MARY ANN EVANS] 1819–1880;
Daniel Deronda (1876)

❧

Yes'm, old friends is always best, 'less you can catch a new one that's fit to make an old one out of.

SARAH ORNE JEWETT 1849–1909;
The Country of the Pointed Firs (1896)

❧

Only solitary men know the full joys of friendship. Others have their family; but to a solitary and an exile his friends are everything.

WILLA CATHER 1873–1947;
Shadows on the Rock (1931)

My friends have made the story of my life. In a thousand ways they have turned my limitations into beautiful privileges, and enabled me to walk serene and happy in the shadow cast by my deprivation.

HELEN KELLER 1880-1968;
The Story of My Life (1903)

❧

Each had his past shut in him like the leaves of a book known to him by heart; and his friends could only read the title.

VIRGINIA WOOLF 1882–1941; *Jacob's Room* (1922)

❧

I have lost friends, some by death . . . others through sheer inability to cross the street.

VIRGINIA WOOLF 1882–1941; *The Waves* (1931)

❧

The heart may think it knows better: the senses know that absence blots people out. We have really no absent friends.

ELIZABETH BOWEN 1899–1973;
Death of the Heart (1938)

❧

The loneliest woman in the world is a woman without a close woman friend.

TONI MORRISON b. 1931; speech (1978)

AGING

Eyes of youth have sharp sight, but commonly not so deep as those of elder age.

ELIZABETH I 1533–1603; letter to Robert Devereux,
Earl of Essex (July 8, 1597) in G. B. Harrison (ed.),
The Letters of Queen Elizabeth the First (1935)

❧

Old age is woman's hell.

NINON DE LENCLOS 1620–1705;
(*La vieillesse est l'enfer des femmes*),
La Coquette vengée (1659)

I have but one prayer at heart; and that is, to have my faculties so far preserved that I can be useful, in *some* way or other, to the last.

LYDIA MARIA CHILD 1802–1880;
Selected Letters, 1817–1880 (1982)

❧

Years do not always make age.

GEORGE SAND [MADAME DUDEVANT] 1804–1876;
The Haunted Pool (1851)

❧

In youth we learn; in age we understand.

MARIE VON EBNER-ESCHENBACH 1830–1916;
Aphorism (1905)

❧

Old age is the verdict of life.

AMELIA E. BARR 1831–1919;
All the Days of My Life (1913)

❧

The dead might as well try to speak to the living as the old to the young.

WILLA CATHER 1873–1947;
One of Ours (1922)

❧

Mr. Salteena was an elderly man of 42.

DAISY ASHFORD 1881–1972;
The Young Visitors (1919)

❧

Nature gives you the face you have at twenty; it is up to you to merit the face you have at fifty.

GABRIELLE "COCO" CHANEL 1883-1971;
Ladies' Home Journal (1956)

❧

Suddenly you find—at the age of fifty, say—that a whole new life has opened before you, . . . as if a fresh sap of ideas and thoughts was rising in you.

AGATHA CHRISTIE 1891–1976;
An Autobiography (1977)

As I grow older and older,
And totter towards the tomb,
I find that I care less and less
Who goes to bed with whom.
> DOROTHY L. SAYERS 1893–1957; "That's Why I Never Read
> Modern Novels" in Janet Hitchman,
> *Such a Strange Lady* (1975)

꒰ꔛ

Old age is like a plane flying through a storm. Once you're aboard there's nothing you can do.
> GOLDA MEIR 1898–1978; in Oriana Fallaci, *L'Europeo* (1973)

꒰ꔛ

The secret of staying young is to live honestly, eat slowly, and lie about your age.
> LUCILLE BALL 1911–1989; in Abby Adams,
> *Uncommon Scold* (1989)

꒰ꔛ

I was thirty-seven when I went to work writing the column. I was too old for a paper route, too young for Social Security, and too tired for an affair.
> ERMA BOMBECK 1927–1996;
> in Dorothy Uris, *Say It Again* (1979)

꒰ꔛ

In a dream you are never eighty.
> ANNE SEXTON 1928–1974; *Old* n.d.

꒰ꔛ

Adolescence is just one big walking pimple.
> CAROL BURNETT b. 1934; on *Donahue* (October 16, 1986)

LIFE

Each thing called improvement seems blackened with crimes,
If it tears up one record of blissful old times.
> SUSANNA BLAMIRE 1747–1794;
> "When Home We Return" (c. 1790)

For what do we live, but to make sport for our neighbours, and laugh at them in our turn?

JANE AUSTEN 1775–1817; *Pride and Prejudice* (1813)

How pleasant it is, at the end of the day,
No follies to have to repent;
But reflect on the past, and be able to say,
That my time has been properly spent.

ANN TAYLOR 1782–1866 and JANE TAYLOR 1783–1824;
"The Way to be Happy" (1806)

Thus strangely are our souls constructed and by such slight ligaments are we bound to prosperity or ruin.

MARY SHELLEY 1797–1851; *Frankenstein* (1818)

It is extraordinary how music sends one back into memories of the past—and it is the same with smells.

GEORGE SAND [MADAME DUDEVANT] 1804–1876;
Story of My Life (1856)

I slept, and dreamed that life was Beauty;
I woke, and found that life was Duty.

ELLEN STURGIS HOOPER 1816–1841; "Beauty and Duty" (1840)

What do we live for, if it is not to make life less difficult to each other?

GEORGE ELIOT [MARY ANN EVANS] 1819–1880;
Middlemarch (1871–2)

. . . it is the greatest of all mistakes to begin life with the expectation that it is going to be easy, or with the wish to have it so.

LUCY LARCOM 1824–1893; *A New England Girlhood* (1889)

Life, like a marble block, is given to all,
A blank, inchoate mass of years and days.

EDITH WHARTON 1862–1937;
"Life," *Scribner's Magazine* (June 1894)

. . . if the production of any commodity necessitates the sacrifice of human life, society should do without that commodity, but it can not do without that life.

EMMA GOLDMAN 1869–1940;
Anarchism and Other Essays (1917)

≈

The years seemed to stretch before her like the land: spring, summer, autumn, winter, spring; always the same patient fields, the patient little trees, the patient lives; always the same yearning; the same pulling at the chain—until the instinct to live had torn itself and bled and weakened for the last time, until the chain secured a dead woman, who might cautiously be released.

WILLA CATHER 1873–1947; *O Pioneers!* (1913)

≈

Total absence of humor renders life impossible.

COLETTE 1873–1954;
Chance Acquaintances (1952)

≈

When I try to classify my earliest impressions, I find that fact and fancy look alike across the years that link the past with the present. The woman paints the child's experience in her own fantasy.

HELEN KELLER 1880–1968; *The Story of My Life* (1903)

≈

Life is a frail moth flying
Caught in the web of the years that pass.

SARA TEASDALE 1884–1933;
"Come," *Rivers to the Sea* (1915)

≈

Life was meant to be lived, and curiosity must be kept alive. One must never, for whatever reason, turn one's back on life.

ELEANOR ROOSEVELT 1884–1962;
The Autobiography of Eleanor Roosevelt (1961)

≈

The trouble with life isn't that there is no answer, it's that there are so many answers.

RUTH BENEDICT 1887–1948; written in 1913;
in Margaret Mead, *An Anthropologist at Work* (1959)

Life is short, and it's up to you to make it sweet.
> SARAH LOUISE (SADIE) DELANY 1889–1999; in Deirdre
> Mullane, *Words to Make My Dream Children Live* (1995)

❧

It is better to be looked over than overlooked.
> MAE WEST 1892–1980; in Joseph Weintraub, *The Wit and
> Wisdom of Mae West* (1967)

❧

Life, the permission to know death.
> DJUNA BARNES 1892–1982; *Nightwood* (1937)

❧

The good die young—but not always. The wicked prevail—but not consistently. I am confused by life, and I feel safe within the confines of the theatre.
> HELEN HAYES 1900–1993; *On Reflection* (1968)

❧

Reality was such a jungle—with no signposts, landmarks, or boundaries.
> HELEN HAYES 1900–1993; *On Reflection* (1968)

❧

Breathe-in experience, breathe-out poetry.
> MURIEL RUKEYSER 1913–1980;
> "Poem Out of Childhood" (1935)

❧

At the end of your life you will never regret not having passed one more test, winning one more verdict or not closing one more deal. You will regret time not spent with a husband, a child, a friend or a parent.
> BARBARA BUSH b. 1925; *Washington Post* (June 2, 1990)

❧

Tremble: your whole life is a rehearsal for the moment you are in now.
> JUDITH MALINA b. 1926; in Toby Cole and Helen Krich,
> *Actors on Acting* (1970)

❧

If life is a bowl of cherries—what am I doing in the pits?
> ERMA BOMBECK 1927–1996; book title (1971)

The future depends entirely on what each of us does every day.
GLORIA STEINEM b. 1934; *Time* (1992)

❧

No one should have to dance backward all their lives.
JILL RUCKELSHAUS b. 1937; speech (1973)

DEATH

How short is human life! the very breath
Which frames my words accelerates my death.
HANNAH MORE 1745–1833; "King Hezekiah," *Poems* n.d.

❧

How horrible it is to have so many people killed!—And what a blessing
that one cares for none of them!
JANE AUSTEN 1775–1817; about the battle of Albuera
[May 16, 1811], (in letter dated May 31, 1811)

❧

In many of our dwellings, the very light of our lives has gone out.
HARRIET BEECHER STOWE 1811–1896;
in James Ford Rhodes, *History of the Civil War* (1961)

❧

Let Death between us be as naught,
    A dried and vanished stream;
Your joy be the reality,
    Our suffering life the dream.

HARRIET BEECHER STOWE 1811–1896;
"The Other World" n.d.

❧

There's little joy in life for me,
    And little terror in the grave;
I've lived the parting hour to see
    Of one I would have died to save.

CHARLOTTE BRONTË 1816–1855;
"On the Death of Anne Brontë" (1849)

In every parting there is an image of death.

> GEORGE ELIOT [MARY ANN EVANS] 1819–1880;
> *Scenes of Clerical Life* (1858)

ॐ

All quiet along the Potomac to-night,
No sound save the rush of the river,
While soft falls the dew on the face of the dead—
The picket's off duty forever.

> ETHEL LYNN BEERS 1827–1879; "The Picket Guard" (1861)

ॐ

Parting is all we know of heaven,
And all we need of hell.

> EMILY DICKINSON 1830–1886;
> "My life closed twice before its close" n.d.

ॐ

This quiet Dust was Gentlemen and Ladies
And Lads and Girls—
Was laughter and ability and Sighing
And Frocks and Curls.

> EMILY DICKINSON 1830–1886;
> "This quiet Dust was Gentlemen and Ladies," c. 1864

ॐ

I think of death as some delightful journey
That I shall take when all my tasks are done.

> ELLA WHEELER WILCOX 1850–1919; "The Journey" n.d.

ॐ

Nothing is more consuming, or more illogical, than the desire for remembrance.

> ELLEN GLASGOW 1873–1945; said in 1937;
> *The Woman Within* (1954)

ॐ

For rain it hath a friendly sound
To one who's six feet underground;
And scarce the friendly voice or face:
A grave is such a quiet place.

> EDNA ST. VINCENT MILLAY 1892–1950; "Renascence" (1917)

Down, down, down into the darkness of the grave
Gently they go, the beautiful, the tender, the kind;
Quietly they go, the intelligent, the witty, the brave.
I know, But I do not approve. And I am not resigned.

> EDNA ST. VINCENT MILLAY 1892–1950;
> "Dirge Without Music" (1928)

ed

The sun has set in your life; it is getting cold. The hundreds of people around you cannot console you for the loss of the one.

> MARIA AUGUSTA TRAPP 1905–1987;
> *The Story of the Trapp Family Singers* (1949)

ed

Dying
Is an art, like everything else.
I do it exceptionally well.

> SYLVIA PLATH 1932–1963; "Lady Lazarus" (1960)

ed

War is not just a victory or loss. . . . People die.

> MAYA LIN b. 1959; architect;
> designed Vietnam Memorial
> in Washington, D.C.

TRUTH, HONESTY, SECRETS, AND LIES

Do not tell secrets to those whose faith and silence you have not already tested.

> ELIZABETH I 1533–1603; in Frederick Chamberlin,
> *The Sayings of Queen Elizabeth* (1923)

ed

The human heart has hidden treasures,
　In secret kept, in silence sealed;—
The thoughts, the hopes, the dreams, the pleasures,
　Whose charms were broken if revealed.

> CHARLOTTE BRONTË 1816–1855; "Evening Solace" (1846)

. . . the truth is the hardest missile one can be pelted with.
GEORGE ELIOT [MARY ANN EVANS] 1819–1880;
Middlemarch (1871–2)

≈

Truth is such a rare thing, it is delightful to tell it.
EMILY DICKINSON 1830–1886;
letter to Thomas Wentworth Higginson (August 1870)

≈

Beautiful faces are those that wear
Whole-souled honesty printed there.
ELLEN PALMER ALLERTON 1835–1893; "Beautiful Things" n.d.

≈

Artistic growth is, more than it is anything else, a refining of the sense
of truthfulness. The stupid believe that to be truthful is easy; only the
artist, the great artist, knows how difficult it is.
WILLA CATHER 1873–1947; *The Song of the Lark* (1915)

≈

Some minds remain open long enough for the truth not only to enter
but to pass on through by way of a ready exit without pausing anywhere
along the route.
ELIZABETH KENNY 1886–1952;
And They Shall Walk with Martha Ostenso (1943)

≈

Nagging is the repetition of unpalatable truths.
EDITH SUMMERSKILL 1901–1980;
speech to the Married Women's Association (July 14, 1960)

≈

Fiction reveals truths that reality obscures.
JESSAMYN WEST 1902–1984; *To See the Dream* (1956)

≈

Cynicism is an unpleasant way of saying the truth.
LILLIAN HELLMAN 1905–1984; *The Little Foxes* (1939)

≈

Every word she writes is a lie, including "and" and "the."
MARY MCCARTHY 1912–1989; of Lillian Hellman,
New York Times (February 16, 1980)

The naked truth is always better than the best-dressed lie.
ANN LANDERS b. 1918; advice column (1991)

SELF-ESTEEM AND SELF-EVALUATION

I have the heart of a man, not a woman, and I am not afraid of anything.
ELIZABETH I 1533–1603; in Frederick Chamberlin,
The Sayings of Queen Elizabeth (1923)

🐦

I am not at all the sort of person you and I took me for.
JANE CARLYLE 1801–1866;
letter to Thomas Carlyle (May 7, 1822)

🐦

Absorbed in the creations of thy mind,
Forgetting daily self, my truest self I find.
MARGARET FULLER 1810–1850; "Flaxman,"
in Julia Ward Howe, *Margaret Fuller* (1883)

🐦

No coward soul is mine,
No trembler in the world's storm-troubled sphere:
I see Heaven's glories shine,
And faith shines equal, arming me from fear.
EMILY BRONTË 1818–1848; "No coward soul is mine" (1846)

🐦

He was like a cock who thought the sun had risen to hear him crow.
GEORGE ELIOT [MARY ANN EVANS] 1819–1880;
Adam Bede (1859)

🐦

To fight aloud is very brave,
But gallanter, I know,
Who charge within the bosom
The cavalry of woe.
EMILY DICKINSON 1830–1886; in Thomas H. Johnson (ed.),
The Complete Poems of Emily Dickinson (1955)

If I ever felt inclined to be timid as I was going into a room full of people, I would say to myself, 'You're the cleverest member of one of the cleverest families in the cleverest class of the cleverest nation in the world, why should you be frightened?'

BEATRICE WEBB 1848–1943;
in Bertrand Russell, *Portraits from Memory* (1956)

ठ•

One can never consent to creep when one feels the impulse to soar.

HELEN KELLER 1880–1968;
The Story of My Life (1903)

ठ•

Let them think I love them more than I do,
Let them think I care, though I go alone.

SARA TEASDALE 1884–1933; "The Solitary,"
Dark of the Moon (1926)

ठ•

No one can make you feel inferior without your consent.

ELEANOR ROOSEVELT 1884–1962;
This Is My Story (1937)

ठ•

You always admire what you really don't understand.

ELEANOR ROOSEVELT 1884–1962;
Meet the Press (September 16, 1956)

ठ•

It is better to be a lion for a day than a sheep all your life.

ELIZABETH KENNY 1886–1952; in Victor Cohn,
Sister Kenny: The Woman Who Challenged the Doctors (1976)

ठ•

When I'm good, I'm very, very good, but when I'm bad, I'm better.

MAE WEST 1892–1980;
I'm No Angel (1933 film)

ठ•

Four be the things I'd been better without:
Love, curiosity, freckles, and doubt.

DOROTHY PARKER 1893–1967;
"Inventory," *Enough Rope* (1927)

You are richer for doing things.

> JESSICA TANDY 1909–1994;
> *New York Times* (September 12, 1994)

❧

Whatever can happen to anyone can happen to me.

> MURIEL RUKEYSER 1913–1980; "Waterlily Fire" (1962)

❧

I've been described as a tough and noisy woman, a prize fighter, a man-hater, you name it. They call me Battling Bella, Mother Courage, and a Jewish mother with more complaints than Portnoy. There are those who say I'm impatient, impetuous, uppity, rude, profane, brash, and overbearing. Whether I'm any of those things, or all of them, you can decide for yourself. But whatever I am—and this ought to be made very clear—I am a very serious woman.

> BELLA ABZUG 1920–1998; *Bella!* introduction (1972)

❧

I restore myself when I'm alone. A career is born in public—talent in privacy.

> MARILYN MONROE 1926–1962; *Ms.* magazine (August 1972)

❧

I've been on a diet for two weeks and all I've lost is two weeks.

> TOTIE FIELDS 1931–1978; in Joe Franklin,
> *Joe Franklin's Encyclopedia of Comedians* (1979)

❧

I'm not fancy. I'm what I appear to be.

> JANET WOOD RENO b. 1938; *People* magazine (1993–4)

❧

I used to think I was an interesting person, but I must tell you how sobering a thought it is to realize your life's story fills about thirty-five pages and you have, actually, not much to say.

> ROSEANNE ARNOLD b. 1953; *Roseanne* (1990)

❧

The people who resent me do so because I'm a woman, I'm young, and I'm a Bhutto. Well, the simple answer is, it doesn't matter that I'm a woman, it doesn't matter that I'm young, and it's a matter of pride that I'm a Bhutto.

> BENAZIR BHUTTO b. 1953; *Newsweek* magazine (July 7, 1986)

SUCCESS, AMBITION, ACHIEVEMENT, AND DREAMS

But the fruit that can fall without shaking,
Indeed is too mellow for me.

> LADY MARY WORTLEY MONTAGU 1689–1762;
> "Answered, for Lord William Hamilton" (1758)

₰

Is *all* that we see or seem
But a dream within a dream?

> FELICIA DOROTHEA HEMANS 1793–1835;
> "A Dream Within a Dream," *Works* (1839)

₰

I have such an intense pride of sex that the triumphs of women in art, literature, oratory, science, or song rouse my enthusiasm as nothing else can.

> ELIZABETH CADY STANTON 1815–1902;
> *Eighty Years and More (1815–1897)* (1898)

₰

Failure after long perseverance is much grander than never to have a striving good enough to be called a failure.

> GEORGE ELIOT [MARY ANN EVANS] 1819–1880;
> *Middlemarch* (1871–2)

₰

Failure is impossible!

> SUSAN B. ANTHONY 1820–1906; speech (1906); in Ida Husted
> Harper, *The Life and Work of Susan B. Anthony* (1908)

₰

Success is counted sweetest
By those who ne'er succeed.

> EMILY DICKINSON 1830–1886;
> "Success Is Counted Sweetest" (1859)

The hope I dreamed of was a dream,
  Was but a dream; and now I wake,
Exceeding comfortless, and worn, and old,
  For a dream's sake.

CHRISTINA ROSSETTI 1830–1894; "Mirage" n.d.

❧

Be true to yourselves; cherish whatever talent you possess, and in using it faithfully for the good of others you will most assuredly find happiness for yourself, and make of life no failure, but a beautiful success.

LOUISA MAY ALCOTT 1832–1888;
"Happy Women," *The New York Ledger* (April 11, 1868)

❧

Fame is a pearl many dive for and only a few bring up. Even when they do, it is not perfect, and they sigh for more, and lose better things in struggling for them.

LOUISA MAY ALCOTT 1832–1888;
Jo's Boys (1886)

❧

Our fathers had their dreams; we have ours; the generation that follows will have its own. Without dreams and phantoms man cannot exist.

OLIVE SCHREINER 1855–1920;
The Story of an African Farm (1883)

❧

The higher one climbs, the lonelier one is.

MARY BARNETT GILSON 1877–?;
What's Past Is Prologue (1940)

❧

The future belongs to those who believe in the beauty of their dreams.

ELEANOR ROOSEVELT 1884–1962; n.d.

❧

I am one of those who never knows the direction of my journey until I have almost arrived.

ANNA LOUISE STRONG 1885–1970;
I Change Worlds (1935)

I don't think necessity is the mother of invention—invention, in my opinion, arises directly from idleness, possibly also from laziness. To save oneself trouble.

AGATHA CHRISTIE 1891–1976; *An Autobiography* (1977)

❧

Please know that I am aware of the hazards. I want to do it because I want to do it. Women must try to do things as men have tried. When they fail, their failure must be but a challenge to others.

AMELIA EARHART 1898–1937; letter to her husband (1937)

❧

Flops are a part of life's menu, and I've never been a girl to miss out on any of the courses.

ROSALIND RUSSELL 1911–1976;
New York Herald Tribune (April 11, 1957)

❧

My success was not based so much on any great intelligence but on great common sense.

HELEN GURLEY BROWN b. 1922;
Words of Women Quotations for Success (1997)

❧

Somewhere out in this audience may even be someone who will one day follow in my footsteps, and preside over the White House as the President's spouse. I wish him well!

BARBARA BUSH b. 1925;
speech at Wellesley College Commencement (June 1990)

❧

Never lose sight of the fact that the most important yardstick of your success will be how you treat other people—your family, friends, and coworkers, and even strangers you meet along the way.

BARBARA BUSH b. 1925;
The Ultimate Success Quotations Library (1997)

❧

If God lets me live, I shall attain more than Mummy ever has done, I shall not remain insignificant, I shall work in the world and for mankind!

ANNE FRANK 1929–1945; *Diary of a Young Girl* (1947)

INJUSTICE AND PREJUDICE;
FREEDOM AND RACIAL HARMONY

It would have cost me more trouble to escape from injustice, than it does to submit to it.

MARIE-JEANNE ROLAND 1754–1793; said in 1793;
in Lydia Maria Child, *Memoirs of Madame de Staël
and of Madame Roland* (1847)

❧

Prejudices, it is well known, are most difficult to eradicate from the heart whose soil has never been loosened or fertilized by education; they grow there, firm as weeds among stones.

CHARLOTTE BRONTË 1816–1855; *Jane Eyre* (1847)

❧

There was one of two things I had a *right* to, liberty, or death; if I could not have one, I would have the other; for no man should take me alive.

HARRIET TUBMAN 1823–1913;
in Sarah H. Bradford, *Harriet, the Moses of Her People* (1869)

❧

How say that by law we may torture and chase
A woman whose crime is the hue of her face?

FRANCES ELLEN WATKINS HARPER 1825–1911;
"She's Free!" *Poems on Miscellaneous Subjects* (1854)

❧

We must educate the heart,—
Teach it hatred of oppression.

CHARLOTTE FORTEN GRIMKÉ 1839–1914;
"Poem," *The Liberator* (Aug. 24, 1856)

❧

So many gods, so many creeds,
So many paths that wind and wind,
While just the art of being kind
Is all the sad world needs.

ELLA WHEELER WILCOX 1855–1919; "The World's Need,"
Custer (1896)

Freedom is always and exclusively freedom for the one who thinks differently.

ROSA LUXEMBURG 1871–1919; *Die Russische Revolution* (1918)

ॐ

The golf links lie so near the mill
    That almost every day
The laboring children can look out
    And see the men at play.

SARAH N. CLEGHORN 1876–1959;
Portraits and Protests (1917)

ॐ

I never let prejudice stop me from what I wanted to do in this life.

SARAH LOUISE (SADIE) DELANY 1889–1999;
Having Our Say (1992)

ॐ

I had felt for a long time, that if I was ever told to get up so a white person could sit, that I would refuse to do so.

ROSA PARKS b. 1913; remark (1955)

ॐ

No other creative field is as closed to those who are not white and male as is the visual arts. After I decided to be an artist, the first thing that I had to believe was that I, a black woman, could penetrate the art scene, and that, further, I could do so without sacrificing one iota of my blackness or my femaleness or my humanity.

FAITH RINGGOLD b. 1934;
Ms. magazine (January 1973)

ॐ

For all the injustices in our past and our present, we have to believe that in the free exchange of ideas, justice will prevail over injustice, tolerance over intolerance and progress over reaction.

HILLARY RODHAM CLINTON b. 1947;
speech (May 18, 1993)

ॐ

What we have to do . . . is to find a way to celebrate our diversity and debate our differences without fracturing our communities.

HILLARY RODHAM CLINTON b. 1947; speech (1993)

Being oppressed means the *absence of choices*.
BELL HOOKS b. 1955; Feminist Theory (1984)

QUEST FOR GENDER EQUALITY

If all men are born free, how is it that all women are born slaves?
MARY ASTELL 1668–1731;
Some Reflections upon Marriage (1706 ed.)

ð

If you complain of neglect of education in sons, what shall I say with regard to daughters, who every day experience the want of it? . . . If we mean to have heroes, statesmen, and philosophers, we should have learned women.
ABIGAIL ADAMS 1744–1818; letter (August 14, 1776);
in Familiar Letters of John Adams
and His Wife, Abigail Adams,
During the Revolution (1875)

ð

. . . I scarcely am able to govern my muscles, when I see a man start with eager, and serious solicitude, to lift a handkerchief, or shut a door, when the *lady* could have done it herself, had she only moved a pace or two.
MARY WOLLSTONECRAFT 1759–1797;
A Vindication of the Rights of Woman (1792)

ð

Nay, start not, gentle sirs; indeed, 'tis true,
Poor woman has her rights as well as you;
And if she's wise, she will assert them too.
SUSANNA HASWELL ROWSON 1762–1824;
"Rights of Women," Miscellaneous Poems (1804)

ð

. . . I know nothing of *man's* rights, or *woman's* rights; *human* rights are all that I recognise.
SARAH M. GRIMKÉ 1792–1873;
Letters on the Equality of the Sexes
and the Condition of Woman (1838)

I have ploughed, and planted, and gathered into barns, and no man could head me! And a'n't I a woman? I could work as much and eat as much as a man—when I could get it—and bear de lash as well! And a'n't I a woman?

SOJOURNER TRUTH 1797–1883;
remarks at the Women's Rights Convention
(May 28–9, 1851)

ᴥ

We hold these truths to be self evident, that all men and women are created equal.

ELIZABETH CADY STANTON 1815–1902; First Women's Rights
Convention, Seneca Falls, NY (July 1848)

ᴥ

The true Republic: men, their rights and nothing more; women, their rights and nothing less.

SUSAN B. ANTHONY 1820–1906;
motto of her paper *Revolution* (1868)

ᴥ

It was we, the people, not we, the white male citizens, nor yet we, the male citizens, but we, the whole people, who formed this Union.

SUSAN B. ANTHONY 1820–1906; speech (1873)

ᴥ

And what is wrong in woman's life
In man's cannot be right.

FRANCES ELLEN WATKINS HARPER 1825–1911; "A Double
Standard," *The Sparrow's Fall and Other Poems* (1894)

ᴥ

Society considers the sex experiences of a man as attributes of his general development, while similar experiences in the life of a woman are looked upon as a terrible calamity, a loss of honor and of all that is good and noble in a human being.

EMMA GOLDMAN 1869–1940; "The Traffic in Women,"
Anarchism and Other Essays (1911)

ᴥ

Men and women should own the world as a mutual possession.

PEARL S. BUCK 1892–1973; *Of Men and Women* (1941)

EDUCATION AND INTELLIGENCE

He who influences the thought of his times, influences all the times that follow. He has made his impress on eternity.

HYPATIA c. 370–415; in Elbert Hubbard,
Little Journeys to the Homes of Great Teachers (1908)

ఎ

The power of generalizing ideas, of drawing comprehensive conclusions from individual observations, is the only acquirement, for an immortal being, that really deserves the name of knowledge.

MARY WOLLSTONECRAFT 1759–1797;
A *Vindication of the Rights of Woman* (1792)

ఎ

The education of females has been exclusively directed to fit them for displaying to advantage the charms of youth and beauty . . . though well to decorate the blossom, it is far better to prepare for the harvest.

EMMA HART WILLARD 1787–1870;
in Anna C. Brackett, *The Technique of Rest* (1892)

ఎ

If the minds of women were enlightened and improved, the domestic work would be more frequently refreshed by intelligent conversation, a means of edification now deplorably neglected, for want of that cultivation which these intellectual advantages would confer.

SARAH M. GRIMKÉ 1792–1873; *Letters on the Equality
of the Sexes and the Condition of Woman* (1838)

ఎ

Teach him to think for himself? Oh, my God, teach him rather to think like other people!

MARY SHELLEY 1797–1851; in Matthew Arnold,
Essays in Criticism Second Series (1888)

ఎ

Be a governess! Better be a slave at once!

CHARLOTTE BRONTË 1816–1855; *Shirley* (1849)

ఎ

I am never afraid of what I know.

ANNA SEWELL 1820–1878; *Black Beauty* (1877)

The whole world of thought lay unexplored before me,—a world of which I had already caught large and tempting glimpses, and I did not like to feel the horizon shutting me in, even to so pleasant a corner as this.

LUCY LARCOM 1824–1893; *A New England Girlhood* (1889)

❧

Only the thinking man lives his life, the thoughtless man's life passes him by.

MARIE VON EBNER-ESCHENBACH 1830–1916; *Aphorism* (1905)

❧

The only language men ever speak perfectly is the one they learn in babyhood, when no one can teach them anything!

MARIA MONTESSORI 1870–1952; *The Absorbent Mind* (1949)

❧

He [Hercule Poirot] tapped his forehead. "These little grey cells. It is 'up to them.'"

AGATHA CHRISTIE 1890–1976;
The Mysterious Affair at Styles (1920)

❧

I have great belief in the fact that whenever there is chaos, it creates wonderful thinking. I consider chaos a gift.

SEPTIMA CLARK 1898–1987; in Brian Lanker,
I Dream a World (1989)

❧

Once I had a professor say to me, "You know you have as much education as a lot of white people." I answered, "Doctor, I have *more* education than most white people."

JOYCELYN ELDERS b. 1933;
New York Times Magazine (January 30, 1994)

WORK AND OCCUPATIONS

To be a king and wear a crown is more glorious to them that see it than it is pleasure to them that bear it.

ELIZABETH I 1533–1603; in Frederick Chamberlin,
The Sayings of Queen Elizabeth (1923)

I shall be an autocrat: that's my trade. And the good Lord will forgive me: that's his.

CATHERINE THE GREAT 1729–1796; attributed

ra

A man who has nothing to do with his own time has no conscience in his intrusion on that of others.

JANE AUSTEN 1775–1817; *Sense and Sensibility* (1811)

ra

Motherhood is the most important of all professions—requiring more knowledge than any other department in human affairs.

ELIZABETH CADY STANTON 1815–1902;
Eighty Years and More (revised edition, 1902)

ra

There's many a one who would be idle if hunger didn't pinch him; but the stomach sets us to work.

GEORGE ELIOT [MARY ANN EVANS] 1819–1880; *Felix Holt* (1866)

ra

No *man*, not even a doctor, ever gives any other definition of what a nurse should be than this—"devoted and obedient." This definition would do just as well for a porter. It might even do for a horse. It would not do for a policeman.

FLORENCE NIGHTINGALE 1820–1910; *Notes on Nursing* (1860)

ra

I am weary of the working,
Weary of the long day's heat.

ALICE CARY 1820–1871; "To Solitude,"
Ballads, Lyrics and Hymns (1866)

ra

Join the union, girls, and together say Equal Pay for Equal Work.

SUSAN B. ANTHONY 1820–1906; *The Revolution* (March 18, 1869)

ra

I felt more determined than ever to become a physician, and thus place a strong barrier between me and all ordinary marriage. I must have something to engross my thoughts, some object in life which will fill this vacuum and prevent this sad wearing away of the heart.

DR. ELIZABETH BLACKWELL 1821–1910;
Pioneer Work for Women (1895)

Work elevates, idleness degrades.

> MRS. H. O. WARD 1824–1899; *Sensible Etiquette of the Best*
> *Society Customs, Manners, Morals, and Home Culture* (1878)

ᕤ

I am not a suffragist, nor do I believe in "careers" for women, especially a "career" in factory and mill where most working women have their "careers." A great responsibility rests upon woman—the training of children. This is her most beautiful task.

> MOTHER JONES 1830–1930;
> *Autobiography of Mother Jones* (1925)

ᕤ

Work is and always has been my salvation and I thank the Lord for it.

> LOUISA MAY ALCOTT 1832–1888; written in 1873;
> in Martha Saxton, *Louisa May* (1977)

ᕤ

Every woman who vacates a place in the teachers' ranks and enters an unusual line of work, does two excellent things: she makes room for someone waiting for a place and helps to open a new vocation for herself and other women.

> FRANCES E. WILLARD 1839–1898;
> *What America Owes to Women* (1893)

ᕤ

A human creature must do human work; and all women are no more to be contented as house servants and housekeepers than all men would be.

> CHARLOTTE PERKINS GILMAN 1860–1935; "The Passing
> of Matrimony," *Harper's Bazaar* (June 1906)

ᕤ

If I didn't start painting, I would have raised chickens.

> GRANDMA MOSES 1860–1961; *My Life's History* (1947)

ᕤ

For an actress to be a success she must have the face of Venus, the brains of Minerva, the grace of Terpsichore, the memory of Macaulay, the figure of Juno, and the hide of a rhinoceros.

> ETHEL BARRYMORE 1879–1959; in George Jean Nathan,
> *The Theatre in the Fifties* (1953)

Personality is more important than beauty, but imagination is more important than both of them.

LAURETTE TAYLOR 1887–1946;
on actors; in Toby Cole and Helen Krich,
Actors on Acting (1970)

ﻉﻉ

I haven't the strength of mind not to need a career.

RUTH BENEDICT 1887–1948; in Margaret Mead,
An Anthropologist at Work (1959)

ﻉﻉ

If you rest, you rust.

HELEN HAYES 1900–1993;
My Life in Three Acts (1990)

ﻉﻉ

Attempt the impossible in order to improve your work.

BETTE DAVIS 1908–1989;
Mother Goddamn (1974)

ﻉﻉ

My grandfather once told me that there were two kinds of people: those who do the work and those who take the credit. He told me to try to be in the first group; there was much less competition.

INDIRA GANDHI 1917–1984; in Carolyn Warner (ed.),
The Last Word (1992)

ﻉﻉ

Always be smarter than the people who hire you.

LENA HORNE b. 1917; interview (1985)

ﻉﻉ

The only thing that separates successful people from the ones who aren't is the willingness to work very, very hard.

HELEN GURLEY BROWN b. 1922; in Carolyn Warner (ed.),
The Last Word (1992)

ﻉﻉ

Behind every working woman is an enormous pile of unwashed laundry.

BARBARA DALE b. 1940;
The Working Woman Book (1985)

WEALTH AND MONEY

Every evil, harm, and suffering in this life or in the next comes from the love of riches.

> St. Catherine of Siena 1347–1380; in Algar Thorold (ed.),
> *The Dialogue of the Seraphic Virgin Catherine of Siena* (1896)

>&

Adversity is solitary, while prosperity dwells in a crowd.

> Marguerite of Valois 1553–1615; *Memoirs* (1628)

>&

If we had no winter, the spring would not be so pleasant:
If we did not sometimes taste of adversity, prosperity would not be so welcome.

> Anne Bradstreet c. 1612–1672; "Meditations Divine
> and Moral" (c. 1655); in John Harvard Ellis,
> *The Works of Anne Bradstreet in Prose and Verse* (1932)

>&

Money speaks sense in a language all nations understand.

> Aphra Behn 1640–1689; *The Rover* (1681)

>&

Come away; poverty's catching.

> Aphra Behn 1640–1689; *The Rover* (1681)

>&

Do you not daily see fine clothes, rich furniture, jewels and plate are more inviting than beauty unadorned?

> Aphra Behn 1640–1689; *The Rover* (1681)

>&

Well! some people talk of morality, and some of religion, but give me a little snug property.

> Maria Edgeworth 1768–1849; *The Absentee* (1812)

>&

A large income is the best recipe for happiness I ever heard of. It certainly may secure all the myrtle and turkey part of it.

> Jane Austen 1775–1817; *Mansfield Park* (1814)

Economy was always "elegant," and money-spending always "vulgar" and ostentatious—a sort of sour-grapeism, which made us very peaceful and satisfied.

ELIZABETH GASKELL 1810–1865; *Cranford* (1853)

❧

I do not own an inch of land,
But all I see is mine.

LUCY LARCOM 1824–1893; "A Strip of Blue" n.d.

❧

Very early in my childhood I associated poverty, toil, unemployment, drunkenness, cruelty, quarreling, fighting, debts, jail with large families.

MARGARET SANGER 1883–1966;
My Fight for Birth Control (1931)

❧

Spend all you have for loveliness,
Buy it and never count the cost.

SARA TEASDALE 1884–1933; "Barter," *Love Songs* (1917)

❧

I have no riches but my thoughts,
Yet these are wealth enough for me.

SARA TEASDALE 1884–1933; "Riches," *Love Songs* (1917)

❧

I've been rich and I've been poor; Believe me, honey, rich is better.

SOPHIE TUCKER 1884–1966; *Some of These Days* (1945)

❧

She was not so much a person as an implication of dreary poverty, like an open door in a mean house that lets out the smell of cooking cabbage and the screams of children.

REBECCA WEST 1892–1983;
The Return of the Soldier (1918)

❧

The two most beautiful words in the English language are "check enclosed."

DOROTHY PARKER 1893–1967; said in the 1920s;
in Leslie Frewin, *The Late Mrs. Dorothy Parker* (1986)

Only the little people pay taxes.

LEONA HELMSLEY b. 1921;
Newsweek magazine (July 24, 1989)

JOY AND SORROW

Oh, how unconstantly our fortune turns.
One hour in joy, the next with sorrow mourns.

MARY DELARIVIER MANLEY 1663–1724;
The Royal Mischief (1696)

ॐ

In chains and darkness, wherefore should I stay,
And mourn in prison, while I keep the key?

LADY MARY WORTLEY MONTAGU 1689–1762;
"Verses on Self-Murder" (1749)

ॐ

Everywhere I see bliss, from which I alone am irrevocably excluded.

MARY SHELLEY 1797–1851; *Frankenstein* (1818)

ॐ

For frequent tears have run
The colours from my life.

ELIZABETH BARRETT BROWNING 1806–1861;
Sonnets from the Portuguese (1850)

ॐ

There is no despair so absolute as that which comes with the first moments of our first great sorrow, when we have not yet known what it is to have suffered and be healed, to have despaired and have recovered hope.

GEORGE ELIOT [MARY ANN EVANS] 1819–1880;
Adam Bede (1859)

ॐ

It is an uneasy lot at best, to be what we call highly taught and yet not to enjoy: to be present at this great spectacle of life and never to be liberated from a small hungry shivering self.

GEORGE ELIOT [MARY ANN EVANS] 1819–1880;
Middlemarch (1871–2)

Better by far you should forget and smile,
Than that you should remember and be sad.

> CHRISTINA ROSSETTI 1830–1894;
> "Remember," *Goblin Market* (1862)

❧

Laugh, and the world laughs with you;
  Weep, and you weep alone.
For the sad old earth must borrow its mirth,
  But has trouble enough of its own.

> ELLA WHEELER WILCOX 1855–1919;
> "Solitude," *Poems of Passion* (1883)

❧

He who is sorrowful can force himself to smile, but he who is glad cannot weep.

> SELMA LAGERLÖF 1858-1940;
> *The Story of Gösta Berling* (1891)

❧

Content is disillusioning to behold: what is there to be content about?

> VIRGINIA WOOLF 1882–1941; diary (May 5, 1920)

❧

I have been in Sorrow's kitchen and licked out all the pots. Then I have stood on the peaky mountain wrapped in rainbows, with a harp and a sword in my hands.

> ZORA NEALE HURSTON c. 1901–1960;
> *Dusk Tracks on a Road* (1942)

WRITING

All letters, methinks, should be as free and easy as one's discourse, not studied as an oration, nor made up of hard words like a charm.

> DOROTHY OSBORNE (LADY TEMPLE) 1627–1695;
> letter (1653)

❧

Let other pens dwell on guilt and misery. I quit such odious subjects as soon as I can.

> JANE AUSTEN 1775–1817; *Mansfield Park* (1814)

If I could I would always work in silence and obscurity and let my efforts be known by their results.

EMILY BRONTË 1818–1848; in Bertha W. Smith
and Virginia C. Lincoln, (eds.), *The Writing Art* (1931)

❧

The writing career is not a romantic one. The writer's life may be colorful, but his work itself is rather drab.

MARY ROBERTS RINEHART 1876–1958; *My Story* (1931)

❧

Originality usually amounts only to plagiarizing something unfamiliar.

KATHERINE FULLERTON GEROULD 1879–1944;
Modes and Morals (1920)

❧

Literature is my Utopia. Here I am not disfranchised. No barrier of the senses shuts me out from the sweet, gracious discourse of my book-friends.

HELEN KELLER 1880–1968; *The Story of My Life* (1903)

❧

A woman must have money and a room of her own if she is to write fiction.

VIRGINIA WOOLF 1882–1941; *A Room of One's Own* (1929)

❧

I love smooth words, like gold-enameled fish
Which circle slowly with a silken swish.

ELINOR WYLIE 1885–1928; "Pretty Words" (1922)

❧

A person who publishes a book willfully appears before the populace with his pants down.

EDNA ST. VINCENT MILLAY 1892–1950; in Leslie Frewin,
The Late Mrs. Dorothy Parker (1986)

❧

Wisecracking is simply calisthenics with words.

DOROTHY PARKER 1893–1967; in Leslie Frewin,
The Late Mrs. Dorothy Parker (1986)

Writing is so difficult that I often feel that writers, having had their hell on earth, will escape all punishment hereafter.

JESSAMYN WEST 1902–1984; *To See the Dream* (1956)

❧

Write about winter in the summer. Describe Norway as Ibsen did, from a desk in Italy; describe Dublin as James Joyce did, from a desk in Paris. Willa Cather wrote her prairie novels in New York City; Mark Twain wrote *Huckleberry Finn* in Hartford, Connecticut. Recently, scholars learned that Walt Whitman rarely left his room.

ANNIE DILLARD b. 1945; *The Writing Life* (1989)

LANGUAGE, THE ARTS, AND CRITICISM

He liked those literary cooks
Who skim the cream of others' books;
And ruin half an author's graces
By plucking bon-mots from their places.

HANNAH MORE 1745–1833; *Florio* (1786)

❧

The book in question is written in a free energetic spirit. It contains a few passages that will offend the fastidiousness of some readers; for they allude to subjects which men do not wish to have discussed, and which women dare not approach.

LYDIA MARIA CHILD 1802–1880; on Margaret Fuller's
Woman in the Nineteenth Century (1843);
from *Broadway Journal* (February 15, 1845)

❧

I'll not listen to reason . . . Reason always means what someone else has got to say.

ELIZABETH GASKELL 1810–1865; *Cranford* (1853)

❧

It was a pity he couldna be hatched o'er again, an' hatched different.

GEORGE ELIOT [MARY ANN EVANS] 1819–1880;
Adam Bede (1859)

If you keep your feathers well oiled the water of criticism will run off as from a duck's back.

> ELLEN HENRIETTA SWALLOW RICHARDS 1842–1911;
> in Caroline L. Hunt, *The Life of Ellen H. Richards* (1912)

૨ે

An unalterable and unquestioned law of the musical world required that the German text of French operas sung by Swedish artists should be translated into Italian for the clearer understanding of English-speaking audiences.

> EDITH WHARTON 1862–1937; *The Age of Innocence* (1920)

૨ે

He can't see a belt without hitting below it.

> MARGOT ASQUITH 1864–1945; of Lloyd George,
> *Listener* (June 11, 1953)

૨ે

The first time you meet Winston [Churchill] you see all his faults and the rest of your life you spend in discovering his virtues.

> LADY LYTTON 1874–1971; letter (December 1905)

૨ે

We are nauseated by the sight of trivial personalities decomposing in the eternity of print.

> VIRGINIA WOOLF 1882–1941; *The Common Reader* (1925)

૨ે

This is not a novel to be tossed aside lightly. It should be thrown with great force.

> DOROTHY PARKER 1893–1967;
> in R. E. Drennan, *Wit's End* (1973)

૨ે

Dance is the hidden language of the soul.

> MARTHA GRAHAM 1894–1991; *Blood Memory* (1991)

૨ે

Art is the objectification of feeling, and the subjectification of nature.

> SUZANNE LANGER 1895–1985; *Mind* (1967)

૨ે

Interpretation is the revenge of the intellect upon art.

> SUSAN SONTAG b. 1933; *Evergreen Review* (December 1964)

The opposite of talking isn't listening. The opposite of talking is waiting.

FRAN LEBOWITZ b. 1946; *Social Studies* (1981)

੨ॕ

[Roger Fry] gave us the term "Post-Impressionist," without realizing that the late twentieth century would soon be entirely fenced in with posts.

JEANETTE WINTERSON b. 1959; *Art Objects* (1995)

NATURE, THE ENVIRONMENT, AND TIME

No time like the present.

MARY DELARIVIER MANLEY 1663–1724;
The Lost Lover (1696)

੨ॕ

Twinkle, twinkle, little star!
How I wonder what you are,
Up above the world so high,
Like a diamond in the sky!

JANE TAYLOR 1783–1824; "The Star" (1806)

੨ॕ

Rocked in the cradle of the deep
I lay me down in peace to sleep.

EMMA HART WILLARD 1787–1870;
"Rocked in the cradle of the deep" (1831)

੨ॕ

Day, in melting purple dying.

MARIA GOWEN BROOKS 1794–1845; "Song,"
A *Gallery of Distinguished English
and American Female Poets* (1860)

੨ॕ

Near all the birds
Will sing at dawn,—and yet we do not take
The chaffering swallow for the holy lark.

ELIZABETH BARRETT BROWNING 1806–1861;
Aurora Leigh (1857)

He who plants a tree
   Plants a hope.

Lucy Larcom 1824–1893; "Plant a Tree" n.d.

શ

Who has seen the wind?
   Neither you nor I;
But when the trees bow down their heads
   The wind is passing by.

Christina Rossetti 1830–1894;
"Who Has Seen the Wind?," *Sing-Song* (1872)

શ

In the bleak mid-winter
Frosty wind made moan,
Earth stood hard as iron,
Water like a stone.

Christina Rossetti 1830–1894;
"Mid-Winter" (1875)

શ

Backward, turn backward, O Time, in your flight,
Make me a child again just for to-night!

Elizabeth Akers Allen 1832–1911; "Rock Me to Sleep,"
Saturday Evening Post (1860)

શ

America! America!
God shed His grace on thee
And crown thy good with brotherhood
From sea to shining sea!

Katharine Lee Bates 1850–1929;
"America the Beautiful" (1911)

શ

If the sight of the blue skies fills you with joy, if a blade of grass spring-
ing up in the fields has power to move you, if the simple things of
nature have a message that you understand, rejoice, for your soul is
alive . . .

Eleonora Duse 1858–1924;
in Toby Cole and Helen Krich,
Actors on Acting (1970)

The kiss of the sun for pardon,
The song of the birds for mirth,
One is nearer God's Heart in a garden
Than anywhere else on earth.

> DOROTHY FRANCES GURNEY 1858–1932;
> "God's Garden," *Poems* (1913)

❧

Nothing natural can be wholly unworthy.

> ANNA JULIA COOPER 1859–1964; *A Voice from the South* (1892)

❧

I like trees because they seem more resigned to the way they have to live than other things do.

> WILLA CATHER 1873–1947; *O Pioneers!* (1913)

❧

Listen . . .
With faint dry sound,
Like steps of passing ghosts,
The leaves, frost-crisp'd, break from the trees
And fall.

> ADELAIDE CRAPSEY 1878–1914;
> "November Night," *Verse* (1915)

❧

Everything on the earth has a purpose, every disease an herb to cure it, and every person a mission.

> MOURNING DOVE [CHRISTAL QUINTASKET] 1888–1936

❧

Time is a dressmaker specializing in alterations.

> FAITH BALDWIN 1893–1978; *Face Toward the Spring* (1956)

❧

Time is the thief you cannot banish.

> PHYLLIS MCGINLEY 1905–1978; "Ballad of Lost Objects,"
> *Times Three: 1932–1960* (1960)

❧

Rivers perhaps are the only physical features of the world that are at their best from the air.

> ANNE MORROW LINDBERGH b. 1906; *North to the Orient* (1935)

In every grain of sand there is a story of the earth.

RACHEL CARSON 1907–1964;
"Our Ever-Changing Shore," *Holiday* (July 1958)

≥●

Shoot all the bluejays you want, if you can hit 'em, but remember it's a sin to kill a mockingbird.

HARPER LEE b. 1926; *To Kill a Mockingbird* (1960)

≥●

Night comes to the desert all at once, as if someone turned off the light.

JOYCE CAROL OATES b. 1938; "Interior Monologue,"
The Wheel of Love and Other Stories (1969)

CULTURE AND POLITICS

My heart turns to and fro,
In thinking what will the people say,
They who shall see my monument in after years,
And shall speak of what I have done.

QUEEN HATSHEPSUT OF EGYPT c. 1501–c. 1482 B.C.;
"Speech of the Queen," in Margaret Busby, (ed.),
Daughters of Africa (1992)

≥●

General notions are generally wrong.

LADY MARY WORTLEY MONTAGU 1689–1762;
letter (March 1710)

≥●

Mine eyes have seen the glory of the coming of the Lord:
He is trampling out the vintage where the grapes of wrath are stored.

JULIA WARD HOWE 1819–1910; "Battle Hymn of the Republic,"
The Atlantic (1862)

≥●

Moral qualities rule the world, but at short distances the senses are despotic.

MRS. H. O. WARD 1824–1899;
*Sensible Etiquette of the Best Society Customs,
Manners, Morals, and Home Culture* (1878)

A leader must stand alone.

MOTHER JONES 1830–1930;
The Autobiography of Mother Jones (1925)

ટ8.

The splendid discontent of God
With chaos, made the world.
And from the discontent of man
The world's best progress springs.

ELLA WHEELER WILCOX 1855–1919;
"Discontent" n.d.

ટ8.

There is no king who has not had a slave among his ancestors, and no
slave who has not had a king among his.

HELEN KELLER 1880–1968;
The Story of My Life (1903)

ટ8.

I want to stand by my country, but I cannot vote for war.

JEANNETTE RANKIN 1880–1973; speech (1917)

ટ8.

The basis of world peace is the teaching which runs through almost all
the great religions of the world. "Love thy neighbor as thyself." Christ,
some of the other great Jewish teachers, Buddha, all preached it. Their
followers forgot it. What is the trouble between capital and labor, what
is the trouble in many of our communities, but rather a universal forgetting that this teaching is one of our first obligations.

ELEANOR ROOSEVELT 1884–1962; said in 1925;
in *Eleanor and Franklin* (1971)

ટ8.

It is better to die on your feet than to live on your knees!

DOLORES IBÁRRURI "La Pasionaria" 1895–1989;
speech (1936)

ટ8.

As the traveler who has once been from home is wiser than he who has
never left his own doorstep, so a knowledge of one other culture should
sharpen our ability to scrutinize more steadily, to appreciate more lovingly, our own.

MARGARET MEAD 1901–1978;
Coming of Age in Samoa (1928)

You cannot shake hands with a clenched fist.

> INDIRA GANDHI 1917–1984; in Carolyn Warner (ed.),
> *The Last Word* (1992)

❧

It is exciting to have a real crisis on your hands, when you have spent half your political life dealing with humdrum issues like the environment.

> MARGARET THATCHER b. 1925;
> speech on the Falklands campaign, 1982

❧

There is no such thing as Society. There are individual men and women, and there are families.

> MARGARET THATCHER b. 1925;
> *Woman's Own* (October 31, 1987)

VARIOUS SUBJECTS / MISCELLANEOUS

What is beautiful is good and who is good will soon also be beautiful.

> SAPPHO c. 613–580 B.C.; "Fragment, 101"

❧

If the people have no bread, let them eat cake.

> MARIE ANTOINETTE 1755–1793; attributed

❧

"Will you walk into my parlor?" said the Spider to the Fly;
"'Tis the prettiest little parlor that ever you did spy."

> MARY HOWITT 1799–1888; "The Spider and the Fly,"
> *Ballads and Other Poems* (1847)

❧

What's the use of watching? A watched pot never boils.

> ELIZABETH GASKELL 1810–1865; *Mary Barton* (1848)

❧

Conventionality is not morality. Self-righteousness is not religion.

> CHARLOTTE BRONTË 1816–1855; *Jane Eyre* (1848)

A maggot must be born i' the rotten cheese to like it.
GEORGE ELIOT [MARY ANN EVANS] 1819–1880;
Adam Bede (1859)

≈

Give me your tired, your poor,
Your huddled masses yearning to breathe free,
The wretched refuse of your teeming shore.
Send these, the homeless, tempest-tost to me,
I lift my lamp beside the golden door!
EMMA LAZARUS 1849–1887; "The New Colossus" (1883)

≈

Beauty is in the eye of the beholder.
MARGARET WOLFE HUNGERFORD 1855?–1897;
Molly Bawn (1878)

≈

If you have anything to tell me of importance, for God's sake begin at the end.
SARA JEANNETTE DUNCAN 1861–1922;
in William Safire and Leonard Safir, *Words of Wisdom*

≈

Why don't you come up sometime, see me?
MAE WEST 1892–1980; commonly misquoted
She Done Him Wrong (1933)

≈

He liked to observe emotions; they were like red lanterns strung along the dark unknown of another's personality, marking vulnerable points.
AYN RAND 1905–1982; *Atlas Shrugged* (1957)

≈

Let us always meet each other with a smile, for the smile is the beginning of love.
MOTHER TERESA 1910–1997; in Barbara Shiels,
Women and the Nobel Prize (1985)

Index of Authors

Abzug, Bella, 37
Adams, Abigail, 43
Alcott, Louisa May, 2, 14, 16, 39, 48
Aldrude, 20
Allen, Elizabeth Akers, 58
Allerton, Ellen Palmer, 34
Angelou, Maya, 17, 23
Anthony, Susan B., 13, 38, 44, 47
Antoinette, Marie, 62
Ashford, Daisy, 26
Asquith, Margot, 56
Astell, Mary, 43
Astor, Nancy, 14
Austen, Jane, 5, 8, 13, 21, 28, 31, 47, 50, 53

Baldwin, Faith, 59
Ball, Lucille, 27
Bankhead, Tallulah, 12
Barnes, Djuna, 30
Barr, Amelia E., 10, 22, 26
Barrymore, Ethel, 48
Bates, Katharine Lee, 58
Baum, Vicki, 15
Beauvoir, Simone de, 4
Beers, Ethel Lynn, 32
Beeton, Mrs., 19
Behn, Aphra, 8, 50
Benedict, Ruth, 29, 49
Bennett, Jill, 15
Benson, Stella, 17
Bhutto, Benazir, 37
Blackwell, Dr. Elizabeth, 13, 47
Blamire, Susanna, 27

Bogan, Louise, 3
Bombeck, Erma, 27, 30
Bonaparte, Elizabeth Patterson, 13
Boosler, Elayne, 7
Bowen, Elizabeth, 18, 25
Bradstreet, Anne, 1, 12, 50
Brice, Fanny, 6
Brontë, Charlotte, 31, 33, 41, 45, 62
Brontë, Emily, 9, 35, 54
Brookner, Anita, 17
Brooks, Maria Gowen, 57
Brown, Helen Gurley, 40, 49
Browning, Elizabeth Barrett, 2, 9, 21, 52, 57
Buck, Pearl S., 19, 44
Burnett, Carol, 27
Burney, Fanny, 8, 12, 20, 24
Bush, Barbara, 30, 40

Carlyle, Jane, 35
Carson, Rachel, 60
Cary, Alice, 47
Cather, Willa, 10, 22, 24, 26, 29, 34, 59
Catherine of Siena, St., 20, 50
Catherine the Great, 47
Centlivre, Susannah, 8, 24
Chanel, Gabrielle "Coco," 11, 26
Child, Lydia Maria, 2, 9, 16, 26, 55
Christie, Agatha, 15, 26, 40, 46
Chudleigh, Lady Mary, 12
Clark, Septima, 46
Cleghorn, Sarah N., 42
Clinton, Hillary Rodham, 42

Colette, 29
Cooper, Anna Julia, 59
Cornelia, 17
Crapsey, Adelaide, 59
Cruse, Heloise, 19

Dale, Barbara, 49
Davis, Bette, 49
Delany, Sarah Louise (Sadie), 30, 42
Diana, Princess of Wales, 15
Dickinson, Emily, 32, 34, 35, 38
Dillard, Annie, 55
Diller, Phyllis, 4
Dix, Dorothy, 14
Dudevant, Madame. See Sand,
    George
Duncan, Sara Jeannette, 63
Duse, Eleonora, 58

Earhart, Amelia, 40
Ebner-Eschenbach, Marie von, 10,
    22, 26, 46
Edgeworth, Maria, 4, 50
Elders, Joycelyn, 46
Eliot, George, 2, 5, 9, 13, 16, 21, 22,
    24, 28, 32, 34, 35, 38, 47, 52,
    55, 63
Elizabeth I, 12, 20, 25, 33, 35, 46
Embury, Emma C., 9
Evans, Mary Ann. See Eliot, George

Fanshawe, Ann, 20
Fern, Fanny, 9, 16
Fields, Totie, 37
Fisher, Dorothy Canfield, 16
Ford, Anna, 4
Frank, Anne, 40
Fuller, Margaret, 5, 35

Gabe, Frances, 7
Gabor, Zsa Zsa, 15
Gandhi, Indira, 49, 62
Gaskell, Elizabeth, 5, 51, 55, 62
Gerould, Katherine Fullerton, 54
Gilman, Charlotte Perkins, 19, 48
Gilson, Mary Barnett, 39
Glasgow, Ellen, 32

Goldman, Emma, 10, 29, 44
Graham, Clementina Stirling, 21
Graham, Martha, 56
Grimké, Charlotte Forten, 41
Grimké, Sarah M., 43, 45
Gurney, Dorothy Frances, 59

Hale, Sarah Josepha, 24
Hall, Hazel, 3
Harper, Frances Ellen Watkins, 10,
    41, 44
Hatshepsut, Queen of Egypt, 60
Hayes, Helen, 30, 49
Hellman, Lillian, 34
Helmsley, Leona, 52
Hemans, Felicia Dorothea, 38
hooks, bell, 43
Hooper, Ellen Sturgis, 28
Horne, Lena, 49
Howe, Julia Ward, 60
Howitt, Mary, 62
Hungerford, Margaret Wolfe, 63
Hurston, Zora Neale, 53
Hypatia, 45

Ibárruri, Dolores, 61

James, P. D., 18
Jewett, Sarah Orne, 16, 24
Jones, Mother, 48, 61

Keller, Helen, 23, 25, 29, 36, 54, 61
Kennedy, Florynce, 7
Kenny, Elizabeth, 34, 36

Lagerlöf, Selma, 53
Lamb, Mary Ann, 17
Landers, Ann, 35
Langer, Suzanne, 56
Larcom, Lucy, 28, 46, 51, 58
Lazarus, Emma, 63
Lebowitz, Fran, 24, 57
Lee, Harper, 60
Lenclos, Ninon de, 25
Lin, Maya, 33
Lindbergh, Anne Morrow, 19, 59
Longworth, Alice Roosevelt, 23

Lowell, Amy, 10, 11
Luce, Clare Booth, 4
Luxemburg, Rosa, 42
Lytton, Lady, 56

Malina, Judith, 30
Manley, Mary Delarivier, 52, 57
Marguerite of Navarre, 12
Marguerite of Valois, 50
McCarthy, Mary, 34
McGinley, Phyllis, 59
Mead, Margaret, 7, 23, 61
Meir, Golda, 27
Millay, Edna St. Vincent, 11, 18, 32, 33, 54
Mitchell, Margaret, 18
Monroe, Marilyn, 37
Montagu, Lady Mary Wortley, 38, 52, 60
Montessori, Maria, 46
Moore, Marianne, 11
More, Hannah, 1, 31, 55
Morrison, Toni, 25
Moses, Grandma, 48
Mourning Dove, 59

Nightingale, Florence, 47

Oates, Joyce Carol, 60
Onassis, Jacqueline Kennedy, 18
Osborne, Dorothy (Lady Temple), 53
Ouida, 22

Parker, Dorothy, 7, 11, 36, 51, 54, 56
Parks, Rosa, 42
Phelps, Elizabeth Stuart, 14
Plath, Sylvia, 33
Porter, Eleanor H., 5

Quintasket, Christal. See Mourning Dove

Ramée, Marie Louise de la. See Ouida
Rand, Ayn, 63
Rankin, Jeannette, 61
Reagan, Nancy, 3

Reno, Janet Wood, 37
Richards, Ellen Henrietta Swallow, 56
Rinehart, Mary Roberts, 54
Ringgold, Faith, 42
Roland, Marie-Jeanne, 4, 41
Roosevelt, Eleanor, 3, 18, 23, 29, 36, 39, 61
Roseanne, 37
Rossetti, Christina, 16, 39, 53, 58
Rowland, Helen, 6, 14
Rowson, Susanna Haswell, 43
Ruckelshaus, Jill, 31
Rukeyser, Muriel, 30, 37
Russell, Rosalind, 40

Sand, George, 26, 28
Sanger, Margaret, 2, 51
Sangster, Margaret E., 22
Sappho, 7, 20, 62
Sayers, Dorothy L., 27
Schreiner, Olive, 39
Sewell, Anna, 45
Sexton, Anne, 27
Shaw, Anna Howard, 5
Shelley, Mary, 28, 45, 52
Sontag, Susan, 56
Staël, Madame de, 1, 21
Stanton, Elizabeth Cady, 38, 44, 47
Stein, Gertrude, 18
Steinem, Gloria, 4, 31
Stopes, Marie, 11
Stowe, Harriet Beecher, 17, 21, 31
Strong, Anna Louise, 39
Summerskill, Edith, 34

Tandy, Jessica, 37
Tanfield, Elizabeth, Lady, 8
Taylor, Ann, 15, 28
Taylor, Elizabeth, 15
Taylor, Jane, 28, 57
Taylor, Laurette, 49
Teasdale, Sara, 3, 11, 29, 36, 51
Teresa, Mother, 23, 63
Thatcher, Margaret, 4, 20, 62
Townsend, Mary Ashley, 10
Trapp, Maria Augusta, 33

Truth, Sojourner, 44
Tubman, Harriet, 41
Tucker, Sophie, 51

Victoria, Queen, 17

Walters, Barbara, 18
Ward, Mrs. H. O., 48, 60
Webb, Beatrice, 36
West, Jessamyn, 34, 55
West, Mae, 6, 30, 36, 63
West, Rebecca, 6, 19, 51
Wharton, Edith, 28, 56
Whitton, Charlotte, 3

Wickham, Anna, 14
Wilcox, Ella Wheeler, 10, 32, 41,
    53, 61
Willard, Emma Hart, 1, 45, 57
Willard, Frances E., 48
Williams, Helen Maria, 8
Willis, Sara Payson. *See* Fern, Fanny
Winfrey, Oprah, 17
Winterson, Jeanette, 57
Wollstonecraft, Mary, 1, 15, 43, 45
Woolf, Virginia, 25, 53, 54, 56
Wright, Frances, 21
Wylie, Elinor, 3, 54

DOVER · THRIFT · EDITIONS

FICTION

THE NECKLACE AND OTHER SHORT STORIES, Guy de Maupassant. 128pp. 27064-5 $1.00
BARTLEBY AND BENITO CERENO, Herman Melville. 112pp. 26473-4 $1.00
THE OIL JAR AND OTHER STORIES, Luigi Pirandello. 96pp. 28459-X $1.00
THE GOLD-BUG AND OTHER TALES, Edgar Allan Poe. 128pp. 26875-6 $1.00
TALES OF TERROR AND DETECTION, Edgar Allan Poe. 96pp. 28744-0 $1.00
THE QUEEN OF SPADES AND OTHER STORIES, Alexander Pushkin. 128pp. 28054-3 $1.50
SREDNI VASHTAR AND OTHER STORIES, Saki (H. H. Munro). 96pp. 28521-9 $1.00
THE STORY OF AN AFRICAN FARM, Olive Schreiner. 256pp. 40165-0 $2.00
FRANKENSTEIN, Mary Shelley. 176pp. 28211-2 $1.00
THREE LIVES, Gertrude Stein. 176pp. (Available in U.S. only.) 28059-4 $2.00
THE STRANGE CASE OF DR. JEKYLL AND MR. HYDE, Robert Louis Stevenson. 64pp.
  26688-5 $1.00
TREASURE ISLAND, Robert Louis Stevenson. 160pp. 27559-0 $1.50
GULLIVER'S TRAVELS, Jonathan Swift. 240pp. 29273-8 $2.00
THE KREUTZER SONATA AND OTHER SHORT STORIES, Leo Tolstoy. 144pp. 27805-0 $1.50
THE WARDEN, Anthony Trollope. 176pp. 40076-X $2.00
FIRST LOVE AND DIARY OF A SUPERFLUOUS MAN, Ivan Turgenev. 96pp. 28775-0 $1.50
FATHERS AND SONS, Ivan Turgenev. 176pp. 40073-5 $2.00
ADVENTURES OF HUCKLEBERRY FINN, Mark Twain. 224pp. 28061-6 $2.00
THE ADVENTURES OF TOM SAWYER, Mark Twain. 192pp. 40077-8 $2.00
THE MYSTERIOUS STRANGER AND OTHER STORIES, Mark Twain. 128pp. 27069-6 $1.00
HUMOROUS STORIES AND SKETCHES, Mark Twain. 80pp. 29279-7 $1.00
CANDIDE, Voltaire (François-Marie Arouet). 112pp. 26689-3 $1.00
GREAT SHORT STORIES BY AMERICAN WOMEN, Candace Ward (ed.). 192pp. 28776-9 $2.00
"THE COUNTRY OF THE BLIND" AND OTHER SCIENCE-FICTION STORIES, H. G. Wells. 160pp.
  (Available in U.S. only.) 29569-9 $1.00
THE ISLAND OF DR. MOREAU, H. G. Wells. 112pp. (Available in U.S. only.) 29027-1 $1.50
THE INVISIBLE MAN, H. G. Wells. 112pp. (Available in U.S. only.) 27071-8 $1.00
THE TIME MACHINE, H. G. Wells. 80pp. (Available in U.S. only.) 28472-7 $1.00
THE WAR OF THE WORLDS, H. G. Wells. 160pp. (Available in U.S. only.) 29506-0 $1.00
ETHAN FROME, Edith Wharton. 96pp. 26690-7 $1.00
SHORT STORIES, Edith Wharton. 128pp. 28235-X $1.50
THE AGE OF INNOCENCE, Edith Wharton. 288pp. 29803-5 $2.00
THE PICTURE OF DORIAN GRAY, Oscar Wilde. 192pp. 27807-7 $1.50
JACOB'S ROOM, Virginia Woolf. 144pp. (Available in U.S. only.) 40109-X $1.50
MONDAY OR TUESDAY: Eight Stories, Virginia Woolf. 64pp. (Available in U.S. only.)
  29453-6 $1.00

NONFICTION

POETICS, Aristotle. 64pp. 29577-X $1.00
NICOMACHEAN ETHICS, Aristotle. 256pp. 40096-4 $2.00
MEDITATIONS, Marcus Aurelius. 128pp. 29823-X $1.50
THE LAND OF LITTLE RAIN, Mary Austin. 96pp. 29037-9 $1.50
THE DEVIL'S DICTIONARY, Ambrose Bierce. 144pp. 27542-6 $1.00
THE ANALECTS, Confucius. 128pp. 28484-0 $2.00
CONFESSIONS OF AN ENGLISH OPIUM EATER, Thomas De Quincey. 80pp. 28742-4 $1.00
NARRATIVE OF THE LIFE OF FREDERICK DOUGLASS, Frederick Douglass. 96pp. 28499-9
  $1.00

DOVER·THRIFT·EDITIONS

NONFICTION

THE SOULS OF BLACK FOLK, W. E. B. Du Bois. 176pp. 28041-1 $2.00

SELF-RELIANCE AND OTHER ESSAYS, Ralph Waldo Emerson. 128pp. 27790-9 $1.00

THE LIFE OF OLAUDAH EQUIANO, OR GUSTAVUS VASSA, THE AFRICAN, Olaudah Equiano. 192pp. 40661-X $2.00

THE AUTOBIOGRAPHY OF BENJAMIN FRANKLIN, Benjamin Franklin. 144pp. 29073-5 $1.50

TOTEM AND TABOO, Sigmund Freud. 176pp. (Available in U.S. only.) 40434-X $2.00

LOVE: A Book of Quotations, Herb Galewitz (ed.). 64pp. 40004-2 $1.00

PRAGMATISM, William James. 128pp. 28270-8 $1.50

THE STORY OF MY LIFE, Helen Keller. 80pp. 29249-5 $1.00

TAO TE CHING, Lao Tze. 112pp. 29792-6 $1.00

GREAT SPEECHES, Abraham Lincoln. 112pp. 26872-1 $1.00

THE PRINCE, Niccolò Machiavelli. 80pp. 27274-5 $1.00

THE SUBJECTION OF WOMEN, John Stuart Mill. 112pp. 29601-6 $1.50

SELECTED ESSAYS, Michel de Montaigne. 96pp. 29109-X $1.50

UTOPIA, Sir Thomas More. 96pp. 29583-4 $1.50

BEYOND GOOD AND EVIL: Prelude to a Philosophy of the Future, Friedrich Nietzsche. 176pp. 29868-X $1.50

THE BIRTH OF TRAGEDY, Friedrich Nietzsche. 96pp. 28515-4 $1.50

COMMON SENSE, Thomas Paine. 64pp. 29602-4 $1.00

SYMPOSIUM AND PHAEDRUS, Plato. 96pp. 27798-4 $1.50

THE TRIAL AND DEATH OF SOCRATES: Four Dialogues, Plato. 128pp. 27066-1 $1.00

A MODEST PROPOSAL AND OTHER SATIRICAL WORKS, Jonathan Swift. 64pp. 28759-9 $1.00

CIVIL DISOBEDIENCE AND OTHER ESSAYS, Henry David Thoreau. 96pp. 27563-9 $1.00

SELECTIONS FROM THE JOURNALS (Edited by Walter Harding), Henry David Thoreau. 96pp. 28760-2 $1.00

WALDEN; OR, LIFE IN THE WOODS, Henry David Thoreau. 224pp. 28495-6 $2.00

NARRATIVE OF SOJOURNER TRUTH, Sojourner Truth. 80pp. 29899-X $1.00

THE THEORY OF THE LEISURE CLASS, Thorstein Veblen. 256pp. 28062-4 $2.50

DE PROFUNDIS, Oscar Wilde. 64pp. 29308-4 $1.00

OSCAR WILDE'S WIT AND WISDOM: A Book of Quotations, Oscar Wilde. 64pp. 40146-4 $1.00

UP FROM SLAVERY, Booker T. Washington. 160pp. 28738-6 $2.00

A VINDICATION OF THE RIGHTS OF WOMAN, Mary Wollstonecraft. 224pp. 29036-0 $2.00

PLAYS

PROMETHEUS BOUND, Aeschylus. 64pp. 28762-9 $1.00

THE ORESTEIA TRILOGY: Agamemnon, The Libation-Bearers and The Furies, Aeschylus. 160pp. 29242-8 $1.50

LYSISTRATA, Aristophanes. 64pp. 28225-2 $1.00

WHAT EVERY WOMAN KNOWS, James Barrie. 80pp. (Available in U.S. only.) 29578-8 $1.50

THE CHERRY ORCHARD, Anton Chekhov. 64pp. 26682-6 $1.00

THE SEA GULL, Anton Chekhov. 64pp. 40656-3 $1.50

THE THREE SISTERS, Anton Chekhov. 64pp. 27544-2 $1.50

UNCLE VANYA, Anton Chekhov. 64pp. 40159-6 $1.50

THE WAY OF THE WORLD, William Congreve. 80pp. 27787-9 $1.50

BACCHAE, Euripides. 64pp. 29580-X $1.00

MEDEA, Euripides. 64pp. 27548-5 $1.00

THE MIKADO, William Schwenck Gilbert. 64pp. 27268-0 $1.50